Portsmout Corporation Transport

Bob Rowe

© 2012 Venture Publications Ltd

ISBN 978 1905 304 479

Contents

SOUTH PARADE PIER, SOUTHSEA.

H.54

Introduction

The story of public transport in Portsmouth, particularly that owned by the City Council (and its predecessors), has been dealt with elsewhere, under various guises, so why this volume now? Well, firstly because operators from Southern England have not figured very frequently among the 63 volumes (to date) in the Prestige and Super Prestige series from Venture publications, and secondly, and quite fortuitously, a photographic collection which contained the basis of a photographic review of the fleet became available to Venture a year or so ago. An appeal in a catalogue of sister company MDS Book Sales solicited a number of offers of help which have been gratefully received and which have made the production of this volume possible. It unashamedly concentrates on the 90 years of municipal involvement although a brief overview to bring the story as far as possible up to date has been appended.

For my part, after my home town of Reading, the transport of the south coast of Hampshire was as familiar to me as anywhere else, due to the fact that an uncle and aunt settled near Fareham after the Second World War and almost all my school holidays were spent with them. Some of the fruits of this influence have already been seen in *Prestige No. 34 (Hants & Dorset)*. Thus, the desolate wastes of Above Bar in Southampton and Commercial Road in Portsmouth were regular reminders to me at an early age of the ravages of war. Early interest was developed, briefly, in the trams of the former town (later to become a city) and the trolleybuses of the latter, which I observed and compared with those in my home town. Regular visits to Bournemouth and also the Isle of Wight completed my road transport education of the area.

On a personal note, work on this volume has recalled many happy memories of visits to Portsmouth. Many journeys commenced by using the Floating Bridge which operated across the mouth of the harbour linking Gosport with Old Portsmouth until the service closed in 1959, and after that on the famous Gosport ferry. I also remember going out on a tugboat from Portsmouth Dockyard in Coronation Year 1953 to see the lines and lines of vessels anchored in the Solent. I had never seen so many ships in one place before, nor have I ever since! I only managed to participate on one trolleybus tour of Portsmouth, in July 1960. My copy of the itinerary from the day notes that tea and a tour of the depot took place at Eastney, and although at the time I made no record of the trolleybus used, it transpires that it was BUT No. 304. It was on this tour that I recall meeting Sam Harrison, the author of *The Tramways of Portsmouth*, for the first time. Other memories which fascinated me about Portsmouth included that right up to the final day of trolleybus operation, some cobbled roads with setts were still being used where the tram tracks remained in situ with merely a coating of tar over them.

After many years of strolling along Southsea seafront and only seeing warships or Isle of Wight ferries coming from the port, the sight after 1976 of a cross channel boat passing Southsea Castle, and seemingly appearing almost as high as the flats at Gosport which it had just passed, was a sight that still brings amazement. Subsequently, less frequent family visits to Portsmouth were usually to take advantage of these continental ferry services.

I make no apology for the fact that because of my own interest in service development there has been a greater emphasis on this aspect than has perhaps been the case in other books in this series. This approach ran into problems in the latter period due to the frequency and extent of service changes which gathered momentum during the 1970s and 1980s. The comprehensive timetable books ceased to be produced after 1980, being replaced by leaflets for individual or groups of routes. The format of Super Prestige books does not permit the complexity of these changes to be covered to a depth consistent with the earlier years and I apologise to the reader for the coverage of this period being sparser.

I could not have produced this book on my own but with the help of a number of key people, principally David Janes, a friend of nearly 50 years; I hope that the final result is acceptable and enjoyable.

Bob Rowe
Doncaster
December 2011

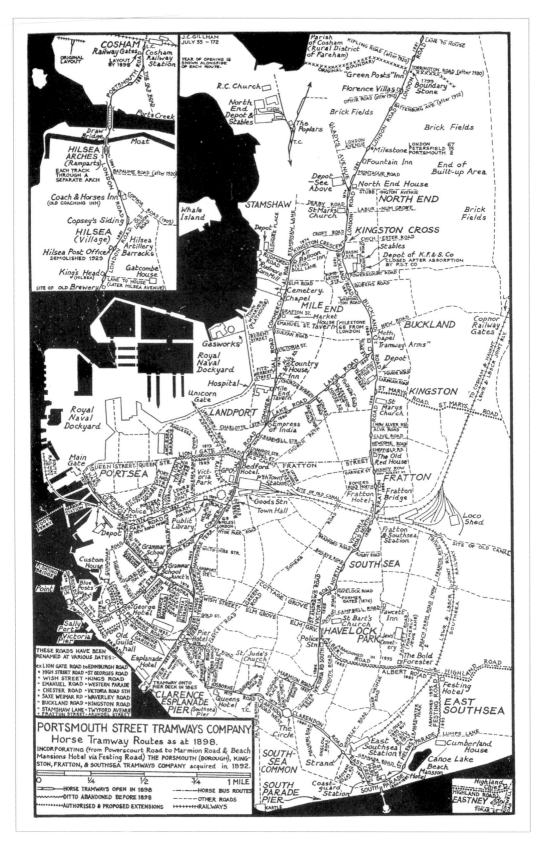

PORTSMOUTH STREET TRAMWAYS COMPANY
Horse Tramway Routes as at 1898.

INCORPORATING (from Powerscourt Road to Marmion Road & Beach Mansions Hotel via Festing Road) THE PORSMOUTH (BOROUGH), KINGSTON, FRATTON, & SOUTHSEA TRAMWAYS COMPANY acquired in 1892.

| 0 | ¼ | ½ | ¾ | 1 MILE |

HORSE TRAMWAYS OPEN IN 1898   HORSE BUS ROUTES
DITTO ABANDONED BEFORE 1898   OTHER ROADS
AUTHORISED & PROPOSED EXTENSIONS   RAILWAYS

4

1 – Early Years

Best known today as a port and naval base, Portsmouth's origins in this dual role can be traced back to its first Charter in 1194. Not long after the town received its first Charter, it became established as Britain's Premier Naval Base and home of the Royal Navy under Henry VIII in the 16th century, whilst in the 19th century it also grew in importance as a seaside resort, largely based on the suburb of Southsea. Geographically, Portsmouth and Southsea are on an island; the local Co-operative society recognised this in its choice of name as the Portsea Island Mutual Co-operative Society. Across Portsea Creek, crossed only by one road bridge until 1941, is Cosham, not originally part of the Borough and nestling under the chalk faces of Portsdown Hill. Today tourism is a significant part of the local economy, although many of the attractions are now linked to its naval history, including the *Mary Rose*, Nelson's flagship *HMS Victory* and the *D-Day Museum*. Perhaps the most prominent feature of the city today is the *Spinnaker Tower* on the Harbour front, opened in 2005.

The first example of organised local transport in Portsmouth dates from 1840 when a horse bus service was recorded as operating between Southsea and North End, probably by the Portsea Island Conveyance Company. This ran, somewhat indirectly, via Palmerston Road, the Dockyard, Queen Street and Commercial Road. By 1857 a further horse bus service was running from Southsea and Old Portsmouth to Landport and by the 1860s other services were provided between the Thatched House, just south of North End junction and Palmerston Road, between the Dockyard and Eastney Barracks and between Commercial Road and the Dockyard. On 8th June 1863 an Act of Parliament was obtained for the operation of trams in Portsmouth which was remarkable as it was the first of its kind to receive the Royal Assent and pre-dated the Tramways Act by some seven years. It was this later Act which subsequently enabled most of the tramway schemes in the country to come to fruition. On 15th May 1865, therefore, the Landport & Southsea Street Tramway Company commenced the operation of the country's first statutory horse tramway service between Landport Station (today's Portsmouth & Southsea Station) and Southsea (now Clarence) Pier. The service was principally provided to link the Isle of Wight ferry with the London & South Western Railway and the London Brighton & South Coast Railway Companys' joint Station at Landport which was originally opened in June 1847. The tramway was intended to permit the through working of railway wagons, which accounted for the unusual gauge of 4ft 7¾ins and which determined the gauge of the subsequent tramways. Initially, step rails were provided, but these were replaced by grooved rails in 1875.

In 1872 the Provincial Tramways Company was formed, which subsequently owned subsidiary companies in Cardiff, Gosport, Plymouth and Grimsby. More pertinently to this history, on 19th May 1873 the Portsmouth Street Tramways Company (which it owned) opened a single-track route from the Point at Broad Street (where it had a depot) via High Street and Cambridge Street to the Bedford Hotel (situated at the junction of Edinburgh Road and Commercial Road) and in September 1874 it was extended to North End (where another depot was owned) via Commercial Road and Kingston Crescent. In another move, perhaps beginning to resemble the 'railway mania' age, the General Tramways Company of Portsmouth opened a line on 18th March 1878 from High Street, Old Portsmouth along Alexandra Road to the original company's line, which it then joined and ran along Kings Terrace and Jubilee Terrace as far as the Pier Hotel and thence along Southsea Terrace, Western Parade and Osborne Road to the Queens Hotel. Inevitably, corporate consolidation arrived, and The Provincial Tramways Company purchased the two companies it did not already own and combined them into a single entity under the Portsmouth Street Tramways name in 1883. This enabled further extensions to be introduced and by 1890 the Dockyard was linked not only with the lines outlined above but reached East Southsea, Fratton, Buckland and Cosham. From 1896 until 1901 a steam tram was operated, using an oil-fired boiler which earned it the title Lifu. It operated mainly, indeed quite possibly exclusively, between Cosham and the Town Hall and was retained by the Provincial company after 1901. The extension of the horse tram services did not, however, result in the curtailment of horse

These two views, both taken in 1899, around two years before the Corporation electrified the tramway system, show horse trams of the Provincial Tramway Company in service. In the view above we see one of the single-deck cars whilst below double-deck cars are in evidence. The photographer was standing on the corner of King's Terrace and Kings Road. Museum Road goes off to the left, Landport Terrace is behind the female pedestrian. (Portsmouth City Museums, both.)

bus expansion and several further routes were opened, including some provided by the horse tramway company.

Reference has already been made to the 1870 Tramways Act, which provided powers for local authorities to acquire tramways and in 1896 Portsmouth Corporation determined to exercise this option. This resulted in the passing of the Portsmouth Corporation Act of 1898 with the effect that it purchased all the lines of the Portsmouth Street Tramways Company (PST) as from 1st January 1901, together with around 60 horse trams. It thus included the short section from Green Posts (the Town boundary at the time) to Cosham. In preparation for this the Council had appointed Mr E Rotter, who had been involved in the construction of cable tramways in Edinburgh, as its first Engineer and Manager, in July 1899. Anticipating the takeover the parent company, the Provincial Tramways Company, obtained powers to extend the system northwards from this point as far as Horndean via Portsdown Hill, Widley, Purbrook, Waterlooville and Cowplain (where the depot was situated). A somewhat unusual state of affairs now occurred, when the Company appointed Mr Rotter as its Engineer late in 1901. His work on converting the horse tramway system to electric propulsion was not yet complete, so a compromise was reached whereby he was retained by the Corporation as a consultant until the work was finished. The Portsmouth & Horndean Light Railway opened on 2nd March 1902 with nine open-top electric trams along a route almost six miles long comprising mostly single-track, a feature that was partially to cause its demise. The Corporation was given running powers over the first mile of the route, but at this stage the Company had no reciprocal rights.

Lest it should be thought that these were the first electric trams in the area, it should be appreciated that once municipal ownership had been established, the Corporation lost no time in electrifying its new infrastructure. The first Corporation electric tram ran in service on 24th September 1901 between Hilsea, North End, the Town Hall and Clarence Pier, the remaining former horse tram routes being converted to electric operation shortly afterwards, giving a route mileage of approximately 14. This service was cut back from Hilsea to North End on 27th September 1901 to save trams which at the time

were only being delivered slowly. Furthermore ,a weak bridge over Portcreek precluded electric trams from operating to Cosham until it had been strengthened when electric services could then commence to Cosham, with effect from 18th April 1903. The last horse tram service was withdrawn in May 1903. To operate these services no less than 80 tramcars were obtained from the Electric Railway and Tramway Carriage Works of Preston. They were all four-wheel open-top 58-seat cars mounted on Brill 21E trucks and were painted in a livery of scarlet and white. A Tramways power station was provided at Vivash Road, Fratton. Following the withdrawal of the horse trams, four of the bodies were rebuilt to a similar style by the Corporation, mounted on Brill trucks and put into service in 1904 as Nos. 81-4, although it would seem that their use was limited. Originally it had intended that these cars would be used as trailers, but when it was realised that approval would not be forthcoming they were motorised. It is ironic that the only surviving Portsmouth tram is one of this quartet. All the new trams were accommodated in the former PST depot at Gladys Avenue, North End, which was considerably rebuilt as a result. The last of the new deliveries received a top cover in 1904 and the following year was decorated to celebrate the visit of the French fleet. The top cover was removed in 1907 and the following year it was used as an illuminated car for the opening of South Parade Pier. The custom of producing illuminated cars was to be repeated throughout the life of both the trams and trolleybuses. The new General Manager, Mr WR Spaven, who had previously been employed as Traffic Manager with Leeds City Transport, and who was to stay for nearly a quarter of a century, was appointed in July 1902, whilst a Mr Lironi, who had considerable experience with electric locomotives, took up the post as Engineer.

The original route from Cosham Railway Station via North End and the Town Hall to Clarence Pier was lettered, appropriately, 'A' and was considerably amended and extended and as route E, also being known as the Outer Circle. Later, and perhaps appropriately, it was given the letter O. There was also an Inner Circle service (it actually operated in a figure of eight) which was lettered H but this was replaced by 1909. Additional extensions were opened in 1909 from Fratton Bridge to Milton and in 1913

An Edwardian view of Town Hall Square with the Town Station in the background. Fortuitously, two consecutively numbered trams have been captured by the unknown photographer; to the left No. 46 is heading for Eastney, while No. 47, on its right, heads for Osborne Road on the Circular service. *(ADPC)*

Approaching the top of Portsdown Hill is Portsmouth & Horndean No. 11. Portsmouth Corporation operated to about half way up Portsdown Hill at Widley Road. *(STA)*

Portsdown Hill

from Stamshaw to Alexandra Park, and also from the Festing Hotel to South Parade Pier and from Milton to Eastney. These final extensions enabled what would be later recognised as the 17-18 service to be introduced, although the terminus was at the Floating Bridge rather than the Dockyard, but at this time was rather confusingly lettered L in one direction and Z in the other! In order to meet this increased demand a further 16 trams, Nos. 85-100, which had direct stairs, entered service in 1907. No more vehicles were to enter the fleet until after the First World War, but its incidence did see the introduction of women conductors to replace the men who joined the armed services. The start of the war also saw the termination of the joint LBSCR and LSWR local railway line from Fratton & Southsea Station, where a branch platform was provided for the service, to the East Southsea Station at Granada Road. The introduction of trams in the

area the previous year undoubtedly hastened its demise, even though a steam rail-car had been introduced in 1903 and two halts opened the following year at Jessie Road and Albert Road. To conclude the review of tramway development a single-deck 'toast-rack' car on a Brill 21E truck was acquired from Southampton Corporation in 1919 and given the fleet No. 104. This car had been new as an open-top double-deck tram in 1900 and had been rebuilt in 1913; it was intended to operate seasonal tours in Portsmouth but it was also used on several occasions as an illuminated tram. For the curious, fleet Nos. 101-3 had been given to works cars. The next trams in the fleet, which arrived in 1920, were, therefore, numbered 105-116 and comprised fully enclosed all English Electric cars which have sometimes been described as 'Leicester' type. The final tram to enter service in Portsmouth did so as late as 1931 as is noted below.

It is August 1930 and two of the quartet of converted horse tram cars, with No. 83 at the front, wait in Park Road by the side of the Guildhall. These cars tended to be used for duplication and specials and are on the centre of three tracks, at one of the few locations where this facility was provided. Behind it, the last of the closed top cars, No. 116, heads for the Dockyard.

BK 2977 (2) is seen above with its original body by Wadham. Note the fleet name and original style of livery application. *(ADP)*

BK 2980 (4) is seen after receiving its 'new' Dodson body. *(RM)*

2 – Motorbuses arrive

Before the First World War there had been some attempts to establish motorbus operation in Portsmouth, but in 1919 an order for ten Thornycroft J motorbuses was agreed by the council; these were fitted with 34-seat open-top bodies built by Wadham and given, predictably, fleet numbers 1-10. Whether the decision to keep the order within the county was by accident or design is not known! These buses were used on a new service between Devonshire Avenue and St Mary's Road via the Dockyard and Arundel Street, largely following what was to become motorbus route C-D, and which commenced on 11th August that year. They had, in fact, been used briefly prior to this for a few weeks on a North End to Piers service. Around this time other bus operators were attempting to establish themselves including Portsmouth & District Motor Services and the Southsea Tourist Company. Southdown Motor Services, which had been formed in Brighton in 1915, and which had linked the two towns from 1920 with the famous 31 service, opened a garage in Hyde Park Road (where Winston Churchill Avenue is today) in 1923. The following year the Corporation more than doubled the size of its motorbus fleet. After a visit to Bournemouth, where a successful seafront service had been operated using 'toast-rack' style vehicles, five similar buses, with Guy J chassis bodied by Wadham and carrying numbers 11-5, were put into use along the Esplanade, on a service that was to prove extremely popular and which was only to cease at the outbreak of war in 1939. The low seating capacity of these vehicles and the nature of the service allowed them to be operated with a driver only.

The other motorbuses to join the fleet in 1924 were seven Dennis 50-cwt single-deckers with Strachan & Brown bodies (Nos. 16-22) which opened a new route connecting South Parade Pier and Cosham via Copnor Bridge. Initially, this was intended to be a temporary arrangement pending the introduction of a tram service along Milton Road and Copnor Road to Cosham but, in the event, it was not until 1952 that a new electric link was introduced. The increased competition from motorbuses was such that from 1st August that year the Corporation agreed to the Provincial Tramways Company extending their service into Portsmouth proper; firstly to the Town Hall and subsequently to Clarence Pier and eventually to South Parade Pier. The previous year a report by the General Manager had proposed purchasing the green trams and the introduction of 'railless vehicles' on services from Cosham to Havant eastwards and to Fareham westwards. Had these far reaching plans come to fruition it is interesting to speculate how later events might have been affected. The report also proposed a new depot, of which more later. In 1925 a dozen more Dennis 50-cwt arrived, numbered 23-34, these being fitted with Dennis bodies and the first pneumatic tyres in the fleet. They were used on extensions to the initial services which reached Tangier Road and Drayton respectively. Borough boundary extensions at this time brought areas of the 'mainland' under the administrative control of Portsmouth Council, but the extension to Drayton did not please the Southdown management which retaliated by increasing the number of journeys into Portsmouth to the detriment of the tram services. There followed several years of dispute over operating areas and agreements which did not hold. Finally, in the early 1930s, the Corporation retreated to Cosham Red Lion and Southdown applied protective fares south of Cosham. The increased Corporation motorbus fleet brought with it a need for more garage accommodation, but as a result of the takeover of Southsea Tourist by Southdown in March 1925, the former's premises at Milton were fortuitously rented.

By 1926 the Wadham bodies on the original Thornycrofts were in need of replacement, presumably because the road surfaces of the time, mainly cobbled streets, had damaged them beyond repair. Eight 34-seat second-hand bodies were, therefore, purchased from London General, having been constructed originally by Christopher Dodson and were fitted to all but a pair of the original motorbuses which received lorry bodies in 1925. At the same time, a solitary AEC B-type (No. B2017, new in 1912) was also purchased from London General and given the fleet number 35. Its original Dodson body was scrapped and a Wadham body from a Thornycroft, cut down to single-deck, was fitted. In London it had been registered LF 9344 but in Portsmouth it carried BK 2342, a number originally issued some time before the Thornycrofts had been first put on the road and originally used by a Corporation

September 1920 and car No. 38, on route Z, negotiates Bradford Junction on its way to Eastney via Milton. *(ADP)*

A few systems were bestowed with a mysterious route 'X', Portsmouth being one of them. Number 44 is in Victoria Road South at the Marmion Road stop. Service 'X' was the partner of service 'B' which ran in the opposite direction. *(ADP)*

This admittedly poor view of one of the Guy J runabouts is included for rarity rather than quality. *(RM)*

The formality of the officials would tend to suggest that this picture from 1925 of No. 23, TP 751, was taken during the hand-over of the first of 12 all-Dennis single-deckers. When new these 26-seat buses were used with a driver only. *(RM)*

lorry. The year 1926 also saw the retirement of Messrs Spaven and Lironi who had both served the department from 1902. Ben Hall, who had previously been with Halifax Corporation, was appointed the new General Manager and like his predecessor was to give a quarter of a century's service to the undertaking.

The year 1927 was an historic one in many respects. Portsmouth assumed City status following the grant of a Charter the previous year and the Town Hall, opened in 1890, assumed the title of Guildhall from this time, which was most appropriate for this impressive building. There had actually been an earlier Guildhall situated in High Street, Old Portsmouth. One wonders if the city fathers had merely renamed it 'City Hall' whether it would have had the same ring about it.

From the introduction of the electric trams the services had been identified by route letters, as has been previously referred to, but from 18th July these were replaced by a route number on trams, and letters were exclusively used on the bus services. Each service had a consecutive pair of numbers or letters allocated to it, the arrangement being intended to assist passengers on a system that had been developed with a significant number of circular or almost circular routes. As far as the writer is aware, this use of a brace of numbers or letters was unique to Portsmouth and was one of the features that gave the City much appeal from a transport point of view. From the same date an agreement was instituted between the Corporation and Southdown Motor Services whereby a protective fare was introduced on company buses south of Cosham, while the Corporation withdrew the previously mentioned Drayton extension, its services thereafter being confined to Portsea Island and Cosham as far as the Railway Station. Despite the boundary extensions already referred to, the result of this 1927 agreement was that the Corporation was unable to provide services for a cluster of its citizens, an aspect that did not escape the ire of said inhabitants and which was to remain an issue for many years.

New vehicles were also introduced in 1927, including a pair of Dennis Es (Nos. 36/7) which were the first forward control single-deckers, and the first covered top double-deckers. They were on Karrier WL6/2 chassis. Numbered 40-7, these had bodies by Brush, and another six similar units (Nos. 48-53) were to enter service over 1927/8,

but with bodies by English Electric, all of which had seats for 60 and which was a significant increase over the 34-seat open-top buses which were withdrawn as a result, the double-deck Karriers being used on the A-B. Credit must be given to the responsible authorities that one of the Thornycrofts was put on one side rather than scrapped and having survived the Second World War and various other vicissitudes it is now an exhibit at the Milestones Museum at Basingstoke. Two Karrier single-deckers were also introduced at this time and like the Dennis Es had Ransomes, Sims & Jefferies bodies. From November 1927 a new E-F service was introduced between Alexandra Park and Eastney. Further Dennis E buses were introduced in 1928 (Nos. 54-61) but this time with bodies by Davidson of Trafford Park, Manchester. These buses enabled the first replacement of a tram service to take place when service 19-20, Fratton Bridge-Clarence Pier (and which had only been introduced in August 1927) was replaced by motorbus route K-L in October 1928.

Clearly the age of the trams was giving some cause for concern but the new General Manager instituted a rebuilding programme in 1929 in an attempt to extend their lives. A brand new tram was also planned which was to materialise in 1931 as number 1 (the original number 1 had been renumbered 53 by this time – the original No. 53 having been withdrawn in 1930), a fully enclosed car on a Peckham cantilever truck with bodywork built in the department's own workshops. Regrettably, its life in Portsmouth was to be short although its subsequent owner, Sunderland Corporation, was to use it until 1953. Sunderland's Manager, Charles Hopkins, astutely collected a selection of modern trams from systems as they retracted and closed down their railed operations completely.

A dozen more single-deckers entered the fleet in 1929 split equally between Dennis EV and Thornycroft BC models with Hall, Lewis (to become Park Royal Coachworks just a few months later) bodying four of each type and Portsmouth Commercial Motors supplying bodies for the balance of the Dennis chassis and Wadham the remaining pair. Fleet number 73 (a Thornycroft) carried the last TP registration mark to be allocated to the department and was destroyed by enemy action in March 1941.

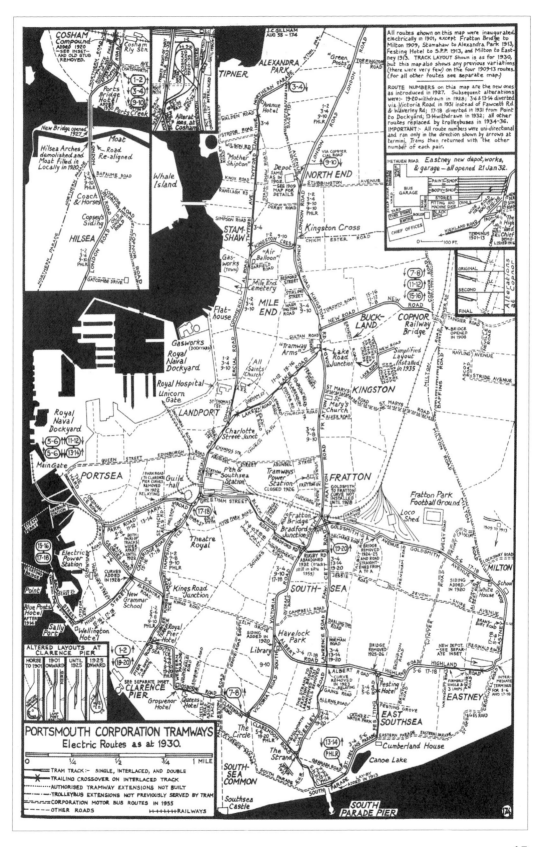

PORTSMOUTH CORPORATION TRAMWAYS
Electric Routes as at 1930.

The first normal-control buses to enter the fleet did so in 1927 when a pair of Dennis Es with Ransomes, Sims and Jefferies 32-seat bodies arrived. This was the first, No. 36, TP 4422. *(RM)*

One of the pair of Karrier CL6s, also with Ransomes bodies, number 38, TP 4812, which were taken into the fleet in 1927 and seated 39. *(RM)*

The first high-capacity double-deckers were 14 Karrier WL6/2, with seats for 60. Number 40, TP 4703, was the first and had a Brush body as did seven more delivered in 1927. It is seen at the Cosham Railway Station terminus opposite Cosham Compound where the tram services terminated. *(RM)*

The only picture that has come to light of a Davidson-bodied Dennis E for Portsmouth is this less than perfect view of No. 54, TP 6864. *(RM)*

In this 19th August 1914 view No. 2 is operating on the Circular service lettered 'O' and will soon be crossing Fratton Bridge. Note the 'All cars stop here' sign on the tramway standard. *(ADP)*

The motorman awaits the bell at South Parade Pier. The restricted visibility to the left as a result of reversed stairs being fitted to these trams is clearly apparent in this picture. Number 10 is operating on route C. *(ADP)*

At Cosham car No. 37 waits to leave for Palmerston Road, Southsea on service 9. No less than six intermediate points are shown on the destination display. Having reached Southsea service 9 will continue back to North End via Commercial Road. *(ADP)*

Dockyard terminus with No. 7 about to leave for Eastney. Many of the buildings in the background disappeared as a result of wartime air raids. *(ADP)*

In 1920 the only trams purchased with top covers, Nos 105-16, were taken into stock. Number 107 stands at South Parade Pier. *(ADP)*

The last new tram for Portsmouth entered service in 1931. It was constructed at North End depot and is seen here at the Festing Hotel junction. *(ADPC)*

Hall, Lewis bodied four Dennis EV chassis for the Corporation in 1929. They had 32-seat rear-entrance bodies and No. 63, TP 8099, was the second of them, seen here in what is undoubtedly a manufacturer's posed picture. *(RM)*

Pictured outside the Guildhall is No. 69, TP 8092, also with a Hall, Lewis body, but this time mounted on a Thornycroft BC chassis.

Wadham also bodied a couple of Thornycroft BCs for the Corporation in 1929, and the final one was numbered 73, TP 8097. It was destroyed by enemy action in March 1941. *(RM)*

The first Leylands were supplied in 1931 and amongst them was a solitary LT2 model, No. 3, RV 238 which was fitted with a Park Royal 30-seat body. *(RM)*

3 – The Thirties

No new buses entered service in 1930, but twelve more arrived in 1931 with chassis from four new manufacturers and two new bodybuilders. Fleet numbers reverted to 1 this year (having reached 73 in 1929) and this was allocated to a Tilling Stevens single-decker registered RV 236, which incidentally carried the first RV mark allocated to the Transport Department. To an extent two of the chassis were by way of being 'experimental', comprising an AEC Regent and a Crossley Condor, which were the first oil-engined buses to be acquired. Both manufacturers offered to convert their buses to petrol engines at their expense after 12 months if the new units proved unsatisfactory and both these double-deckers were bodied by Short Brothers of Rochester. Leyland was another new supplier, providing the first of the ubiquitous Titan TD1 model to Portsmouth, a model which its manufacturer was to allege was terminal for trams. Bodies were by a mixture of Short and Park Royal. The AEC took the fleet number of the second-hand B-type and the Crossley followed on from the 1929 deliveries.

For those of you wondering why Portsmouth Council commenced using RV in 1931 after first using BK and then completing TP, use of which had commenced in 1924, the answer is that all marks containing a 'V' were initially reserved for use by Scottish authorities. When it became clear that a heavier demand existed elsewhere, these '-V' marks were allocated to the various issuing offices between 1928 and 1932.

This decade was to see significant changes for the Transport Department. A concession in the agreement between the Corporation and Southdown permitted the extension of services to the Red Lion at Cosham from 1st January 1932, but the major event of that year was the opening of a new depot and offices at Eastney on 21st January 1932 by the Lord Mayor, Alderman FG Foster. For some considerable time the Transport Committee had been seeking to obtain a site suitable as a central depot and eventually were able to secure around three acres off Highland Road which had formerly been used as a combination of old dwellings in Eastney Road, which were demolished, and land from long gardens of properties in Highland and Methuen Roads. It was adjacent to the existing tramway and, as was reported at the time, had a solid dry gravel bed. Much of the work was carried out by direct labour under the watchful eye of Ben Hall and the new premises provided the whole of the repair and maintenance facilities for both trams and motorbuses. The Transport Department offices were also based on the site, being relocated from the Guildhall. Running repairs continued to be carried out at North End depot, which now accommodated motorbuses as well as trams, having been the site originally used in horse tram days. The opening of Eastney depot permitted the closure of four locations previously used for motorbus storage and was said to have significantly reduced dead mileage. No less than 40 new motorbuses entered service in 1932, so the new premises were undoubtedly welcome. These new vehicles replaced all of the normal control Dennis single-deckers in the fleet, an indication perhaps that greater capacity was now required as all the new buses were 50-seat double-deckers, all with bodies by English Electric of Preston, successors to the Electric Railway and Carriage Company which had built the large order for tramcars. There were ten TSM E60A6 models, ten more Leyland TD1s and 20 Crossley Condors. These latter buses cost £1,075 each for the chassis and £690 each for the bodies. As far as Crossley was concerned, the previous year's 'demonstrator' had obviously proved inspiring to the department, but, trolleybuses apart, it was to be 37 years before more AECs were obtained. July 1932 saw the introduction of a new single-deck M-N to serve the new municipal airport, running as a half-hourly summer season service from Clarence Pier via the seafront, Eastney, Milton and Eastern Road. As part of a busy year Alderman Foster was also involved in the City Airport opening and took a flight over the city courtesy of Imperial Airways on 2nd July. The final decision of 1932 which was to have far-reaching implications was that taken by the Transport Committee in October, when it agreed to the introduction of an experimental trolleybus service between Cosham and Southsea, after two years of deliberation.

For its 1933 deliveries the department returned to Leyland, twelve TD2 models with, predictably, English Electric bodies, entering service that year. These were the first diesel-engined Leylands in the fleet. They were used mainly to convert routes E-F

Tramway & Bus Developments at Portsmouth.

Transport Department's New Offices,

Depot, Garage and Works.

On January 21 the Lord Mayor of Portsmouth, Mr. F. G. Foster, and the Lady Mayoress officially opened the new tramway offices, depot, omnibus garage and works that have been constructed at Eastney for the Corporation Transport Department. The new facilities have been an urgent need of the department for a long time, for since the war the activities of the transport committee have greatly increased. Until the close of the war the Corporation provided only tramway services with a total route length of 17.5 miles ; but in 1918 the Corporation decided to supplement the existing services by the introduction of omnibuses, and in the following year the first omnibus was put in service. With the development of residential areas and the increased demands for transport facilities, the committee, which throughout the history of the undertaking has pursued a wisely progressive policy, have opened new routes from time to time. To-day, in addition to the tramways, the department provides an omnibus service through approximately 26 miles of streets. The fleet of vehicles has been gradually increased until there are now 80 omnibuses, and the number is shortly to be enlarged by 14 new vehicles of the latest design now under construction. The fleet has, in fact, increased so rapidly that the requirements of the transport department have in the meantime outgrown the facilities necessary for efficient and economic maintenance of the rolling stock. While the tramway running shed at North End sufficed to house the tramcars, the machine shop and facilities for repairs had become inadequate. As the vehicles were housed in temporary accommodation at four different points within the city, repairs and maintenance in recent years have been carried on under great difficulties.

The selection of the site for the new depot had been under the consideration of the committee for some time, but it was only comparatively recently that it became practicable for the Corporation to acquire the particular site at Eastney which the committee desired to obtain as it is adjacent to the tramways and has a good solid gravel bed. The entire site occupies three acres.

After a careful survey of the plot had been made, Mr. Ben Hall, the general manager and engineer, prepared a general design of the building and layout for the depot, and on this as a basis a specification was prepared. The arrangements enable the whole of the repair and reconstruction of omnibus and tramcar vehicles, other than ordinary running repairs, to be centralised under one roof, thus securing greatly increased economy. The transference of the offices to the new building adjacent to the works will also add greatly to the convenience and economy of administration. The present North End depot will be maintained as a running shed, and a portion of the fleet of tramcars and omnibuses will be garaged at North End, but the remainder will be housed at Eastney, an arrangement which will considerably reduce dead mileage.

As will be seen from the block plan, the depot proper is divided into three sections. At the east end are the tramway running and repair sheds, and at the west end the omnibus service garage, while between the two are arranged the workshops comprising paint shops, body building, and repair shops, ample general stores, upholstering shop, magneto and accumulator repair shop, and foreman's offices—from which a view of the whole interior may be obtained—machine and fitters' shop, armature and electric repair shop, and blacksmiths' shop.

The transport department itself carried out the necessary excavations by direct labour, and the levelling of the site, which originally had a flow of 3 ft. 9 in. from the south to the north side, and the laying of the concrete basis for the steel stanchions at depths from 4 ft. to 10 ft. The whole of the floor, and the concrete of the car repair pits, are reinforced to carry several lines of track. The bridging, as will be seen from the accompanying photographs, is constructed on the viaduct principle arranged to give access to the trucks of the tramcars and free movement of the men from one line of track to another. The transport department designed and laid down the complete draining system. This is in two sections. The tram shed and workshops drain into the main sewer in the Eastney Road, and the omnibus garage in Middleton Road. Special drain traps are introduced in the pipe lines to intercept any leakage of petrol that may occur. The very adequate lighting installation was installed by the employees of the department.

The area covered by the main buildings is approximately 1⅜ acres in extent, and 400 tons of steel have been used in the girder construction of the skeleton. At the western portion of the building the ample space used for the omnibus garage has a clear span of 120 ft. and a length of 200 ft. This provides an unobstructed were supplied by Mellowes, Ltd. The principal feature is the patent lead coated rustless glazing bars. The glass sheets are all steel wire mesh, reinforced so that in the event of an accident occurring in which the glass is broken, there is no risk of pieces falling to the danger below. The steel mesh screens and the steel armouring of the floor was supplied by Estler Bros., Ltd. The concrete floor surfacing of steel-crete, which is dustless and waterproof, was supplied by Kendell's Paving Co., Ltd. The heating installation is of the accelerated low pressure hot water system incorporating two flue smoke tube dry back boiler units, which are capable of maintaining an average temperature throughout the building of up to 65° F.

The petrol installation consists of four metering filled columns supplied by a motor-driven pump from three underground tanks each of 5,000 gallons capacity, and each capable of delivering petrol at four filling points to the omnibus tanks at the rate up to 20 gallons per minute.

The spacious office building fronting on Highland Road has been designed by Mr. H. J. Dyer, a Portsmouth architect. It is in the neo-Georgian style, and has an attractive elevation with a main doorway constructed wholly of Portland stone. The remainder of the front and parts of the side elevations are of multi-coloured kiln bricks with Portland stone dressings. Within the main entrance are the Tramways War Memorial and Roll of Honour. Here also is a mural tablet inscribed with the names of Sir John Timpson, chairman, and other members of the Tramways Committee. On the ground floor are a public inquiry office, telephone room, rooms for the traffic superintendent, inspectors, lost property and uniform stores, while on the first floor are the administrative suite with the committee and general manager's rooms, general office, and general stationery store. In addition, on the ground floor, grouped around

A Steel Mesh Screen Enclosing a Section of the Stores.

a central circulation area for employees, are the cashier's department, including cashier's clerks, wages, cash counter, and strong room, and a separate ticket department. All the facilities of a modern office building are provided, including central heating with oil fuel, ventilation, electric light and power, gas and

telephone services. Synchronised electric clocks are placed in all departments with the master clock in the entrance.

For the particulars given in the foregoing description of the depot and works we are indebted to Mr. Ben Hall, general manager and engineer of Portsmouth

Conductors' Paying-in Room with Strong Room Beyond.

Transport Department, whose enterprising management has received well merited praise from the chairman and other members of the Transport Committee.

Diagrammatic Layout of New Buildings.

The new buildings were formally opened on January 21, by the Lord Mayor and Lady Mayoress (Alderman F. J. and Mrs. Foster). Before the opening ceremony Sir John Timpson, Chairman of the Transport Committee, welcomed the visitors, who were conducted round the shops by the engineer and manager, Mr. Ben Hall. Subsequently Sir John Timpson, in asking the Lady Mayoress to open the doors of the main entrance, said the occasion was a landmark in the history of the Corporation Transport undertaking. Within the entrance hall the Lord Mayor unveiled a mural tablet which records his opening of the building and contains the names of the chairman, Sir John Timpson, and the vice-chairman, Mr. A. E. Hooper, and other members of the Transport Committee. After the opening the Lord Mayor entertained a large company, including members of the Town Council and many other guests, to tea. In thanking the Lord Mayor for his hospitality, Sir John Timpson alluded to the fact that the Lord Mayor was chairman of the Tramways Committee when the Corporation decided to acquire the undertaking, and that he always had taken a keen interest in the work of the Department.

There were also seven TD1 double-deckers new in 1931, five of which had bodies supplied by Short, as illustrated by No. 5, RV 242. Although now wearing post-war livery, the Short bodies retained the white band under the lower deck windows. It is picking up outside Southdown's iconic Hilsea garage in this post-1950 view. *(RM)*

The other pair of 1931 TD1s were bodied by Park Royal. In this classic view from the bodybuilder, No. 8, RV 716, displays the pre-war style of livery. *(RM)*

The other Park Royal TD1, No. 7, RV 715 is seen post-war at South Parade Pier without the white band beneath the lower deck windows.

This Leyland Titan TD2, RV 3411, dating from 1933, has survived after being used for many years as a tower wagon and towing vehicle. It later became part of the Portsmouth Museum's collection. It is seen here on Southsea Common in the 1980s with Bournemouth vehicles in the background. *(STA)*

Another traditional AEC official view shows No. 35, RV 719, the only AEC Regent supplied to the Corporation and delivered in 1931. This was the first 'oil-engined' (ie diesel) bus bought by the Transport Department, but it did not find favour, unlike No. 74, RV 720, a Crossley Condor fitted with a Short body, which was to lead to further orders of this type. This particular bus was converted to a breakdown lorry on withdrawal from passenger service in 1947, and on retirement from this role in 1971 entered the ranks of preserved vehicles. *(RM)*

The 1932 deliveries were all bodied by English Electric, and No. 78, RV 1141, was one of ten TSM E6OA6 models supplied. *(ABC)*

Post-war the livery on the TSMs was also modified and No. 77, RV 1137 is seen here in Park Road at the side of the Guildhall. *(RM)*

The successful operation of No. 74 led to 20 more Crossley Condors entering the fleet in 1932, all with English Electric bodies. Number 111, RV 2006, is seen before delivery.

The first diesel-engined buses supplied by Leyland arrived in 1933. They were 12 TD2s with English Electric bodies. The first of the batch, No. 16, RV 3410, is seen here in Gladys Avenue passing North End depot. It is on service F to Alexandra Park in 1951, which would be replaced by trolleybus service 15 two years later. *(ABC)*

Another of the 1933 Leyland TD2s is seen at the terminus of route E outside Eastney depot. *(RM)*

The bomb sites of Wickham Street near the Dockyard Main Gate form the backdrop to No. 19, RV 3413, awaiting the Dockyard outmuster. *(ABC)*

and I-J to double-deck operation, the latter service having been considerably extended in December 1931 so that it operated between Green Lane and South Parade Pier via Stubbington Avenue and Fawcett Road, but the increase in the availability of this type of bus also saw the Leylands used on the C-D, which had been extended to Eastney Road. The major event of 1934 was the introduction of trolleybuses, although tram rebuilding was still underway. Route 3-4 from Cosham Railway Station to South Parade Pier via North End, Fratton Road, Fawcett Road and The Strand was chosen for the 'experiment', and 15 eclectic electric vehicles were ordered. There were half-a-dozen AECs (four two-axle and two three-axle); four Sunbeams (two of each); three Leylands (all two-axle) and two Karriers (both two-axle). Bodies were by English Electric save for one of the three-axle AECs, one two-axle and one three-axle Sunbeam and one Karrier, which had Metro-Cammell bodywork. All the Metro-Cammell examples were delivered first, followed by the three Leylands by the end of July so that driver training could commence. In fact, the balance of the 15 new trolleybuses did not start arriving until after the service had been introduced, the final three not arriving until the middle of August. They were numbered in a new series from No. 1, although four years later all the trolleybuses were renumbered by the addition of 200 to the fleet number. Such a large experimental fleet seems to have been a genuine attempt to compare types and very few other operators introducing trolleybuses indulged in similar testing to such an extent. The trolleybuses quickly established themselves as the preferred form of transport for the future and a decision was taken to complete the conversion of tram services within two years, rather then the ten years as originally proposed.

The trolleybus service was introduced on Saturday 4th August 1934 and on the same day bus route I-J was reorganised to run on weekdays from Cosham, Red Lion via Green Lane and Victoria Road to Palmerston Road and thence back to Green Lane via Guildhall and in this new form it replaced the tram 9-10. Two days later the August Bank Holiday occurred, always an extremely busy day for the department. Tram service 1-2 between Cosham and Clarence Pier was replaced by motorbus service O-P from October 1934, this leaving only the Horndean

trams running regularly north of North End although Corporation cars still ran to Cosham for special events as late as October 1935. Since a service of trams between Horndean and Cosham was hopelessly uneconomic against the through-running Southdown buses, the Provincial company sold the goodwill of the service, such as it was, to Southdown and the green trams ceased to run after 9th January 1935. This did not bring to an end completely the operation by the Provincial company in the area, as its emerald buses continue to ply in the Fareham and Gosport area for another 34 years. The conversion of the remainder of tram route 3-4, from South Parade Pier to Alexandra Park via Festing Road, Albert Road, Guildhall and Commercial Road was the next stage and nine AEC 661T trolleybuses with English Electric bodies were ordered for the purpose and became Nos. 16-24. This last of these had actually been on display at the 1935 Commercial Motor Show and had a different style of trolley base. On 3rd November 1935, with the conversion to trolleybuses, the opportunity was taken to extend service 3-4 from Alexandra Park along Northern Parade to Cosham, this being the first time that trolleybuses served a route not previously covered by trams. This new service also required the roadway beneath the railway at Portsmouth and Southsea Station to be lowered to accommodate the trolleybuses. The intention to extend trolleybus services from Cosham Railway Station to Cosham Red Lion resulted in the decision to distinguish between services terminating at, but not starting from, these two locations by allocating a suffix A to the Railway Station services. Thus, on 3rd November 1935, the existing 3-4 service became 3-4A and the new service 3A-4.

July 1935 saw 16 more motor buses begin to enter the fleet, this time of the Leyland TD4 variety, a dozen of them carrying the last English Electric bodies to be delivered to the Corporation. These introduced a new destination screen layout which, apart from the utility Daimlers, was carried by all buses and trolleybuses until 1972. The balance had Leyland's own bodywork. Four of the English Electric examples were to have an extended life when they were converted to open-top for use on the seafront Service in the 1950s. The new Leylands found themselves working on a revised K-L service which had been extended from

The second of the quartet of English Electric AEC 661Ts is seen here in post-war days at Cosham, long after it acquired fleet number 202, RV 4650, Also, by this time, the windscreen has been modified, which must have been a boon to taller drivers!

A trio of English Electric-bodied Leyland TBD2s were part of the initial 15 strong fleet which inaugurated the trolleybus service in 1934. Seen on driver instruction duties is No. 6, RV 4654. Note the window above the off-side windscreen to assist the driver's view of the overhead. *(STA)*

The body on Karrier E4 No. 211 was by Metro-Cammell, and although built with five-bay construction, tended to look more ancient than the English Electric example. Having arrived at Cosham Compound in early post-war days the destination screen havdalready been changed for the next journey to South Parade Pier (pre-war screens are still carried). *(ADP)*

There were only four three-axle trolleybuses in the original experimental fleet of 15 trolleybuses, two AECs and two Sunbeams. Number 15 was one of the AEC 663T models, this example having Metro-Cammell bodywork whereas the other AEC had bodywork by English Electric. It is seen in September 1934, a matter of only weeks old, operating on the then sole trolleybus route. *(GAT)*

Another dozen Leyland/English Electric double-deckers arrived in 1935, this time TD4 models. Four of this batch were to receive fame and significant longevity after conversion to open-top in the 1950s. Over the years football traffic to Fratton Park was to provide work for the department. No. 119, RV 6362 is caught on such a duty. *(ABC)*

For the balance of the 1935 motorbus orders Portsmouth turned to Leyland for bodywork and four TD4s with slightly dated six-bay construction and V-front style entered service. It is understood that problems were experienced with this type of body which required some rebuilding, including the Portsmouth examples, after which they gave many years reliable service. The last of the batch, No. 130, RV 6373, crosses Guildhall Square. *(RM)*

Fratton Bridge to Hayling Avenue the day the first trolleybuses were introduced as a replacement for the 7-8 tram; on 3rd November 1935 it was further extended to provide a Hayling Avenue to Alexandra Park via Osborne Road service. The Silver Jubilee celebrations for King George V and Queen Mary in 1935 was the opportunity for a decorated tram to appear to mark the event but it was probably the last occasion when such a celebration took place. The tram involved was the unique number 104, whose toast-rack body had been rebuilt in 1933 to resemble the hull of a boat and it was then used in August that year in connection with Navy Week, supporting naval charities. In this form it was used for the Silver Jubilee. At the end of 1935 trolleybus No. 20 was loaned to Brighton Corporation who were considering the introduction of trolleybuses at that time; it was used on a length of overhead erected for test purposes along Union Road. Although it would be four more years before trolleybus operation was to commence in that Sussex town its first 44 trolleybuses were also to be AEC 661Ts. To complete the conversion of the tram services, orders were placed for no less than 76 more trolleybuses. Chassis were again to be provided by AEC but this time the body contract went to Craven of Sheffield, another company, like English Electric, with a long history of tramcar construction. The body contract for 30 more Leyland TD4s, Nos. 131-160, the largest single order for motorbuses up to that time, was also placed with Craven; and were identical bodies, apart from the necessary differences between full-front trolleybuses and half-cab motorbuses; these were to be the final double-deck motorbuses delivered before the outbreak of war.

The trolleybus conversion programme continued on 1st October 1936 when the 1-2 from Cosham Red Lion to Clarence Pier saw trolleybuses introduced, replacing the O-P motorbuses which in turn had replaced the trams on service 1-2 two years earlier. It is believed that the 3A-4 and possibly the 3-4A were extended to Cosham Red Lion at this time as 3-4 and 4-3 respectively, but for a very limited period.

These were followed a month later on 1st November by the 11-12 and 15-16 conversions, both of which terminated at Copnor Bridge and which operated to the Dockyard and Floating Bridge respectively. This latter terminal

point was unique in employing a reverser at Broad Street, trolleybuses reversing into East Street. The Floating Bridge itself was a chain-guided steam driven vehicle ferry which ran across the mouth of the harbour and linked Gosport with Old Portsmouth. The final tram to trolleybus changeover took place on Tuesday 10th November 1936 when the 5-6 and 17-18, which served the Eastney/Milton areas, were converted; some 27 years later these services were to be the last to operate trolleybuses. Four sombrely decorated trams made the final journey to Eastney depot. A few months earlier, in June 1936, the name of the undertaking had officially been changed from Portsmouth Corporation Tramways to City of Portsmouth Passenger Transport Department (CPPTD). The last of the 76 new trolleybus order did not in fact enter service until May 1937 and within a year were to receive their new fleet numbers. It is said that with the rear of the more modern motorbuses looking very similar to that of the new trolleybuses, overtaking of one trolleybus by another was not unusual with serious consequences (with lettered route numbers for motorbuses and numbered ones for trolleybuses one has to wonder at this alleged carelessness) but it is further recorded that the then newly arrived, in November 1937, Chief Assistant Engineer, one CT Humpidge, was charged with resolving this problem, and solved it by adding 200 to the trolleybus fleet numbers, which duly took place early in April 1938. Chacely Humpidge subsequently moved to Liverpool as Superintendent at the famous Edge Lane Works, later becoming General Manager at Bradford before ending his career in a similar position at Sheffield. A more pragmatic view of this renumbering exercise suggests that it was done for administrative purposes as much as any other reason as buses and trolleybuses with the same fleet numbers must have been confusing.

As previously mentioned, the newest tram, number 1, was sold to Sunderland; one other tram, number 84, was put aside to join the Thornycroft motorbus. As a converted horse tram it was of some interest, but as representative of the rest of the fleet, of which no less than 80 trams had been identical, it was not! Further fine tuning of the motorbus services took place in 1936 when route K-L was extended to Stride Avenue from 2nd March and a new single-deck O-P was introduced

The last trolleybus to be delivered with an English Electric body, in 1935, was No. 224, RV 6382, seen here at the South Parade Pier terminal. This was also the last of this order to remain in service. *(STA)*

Having placed orders with Craven of Sheffield for a significant number of trolleybuses (they were eventually to total 76 units) it was perhaps not surprising that the same firm should supply bodies for motorbuses. The order was for 30 and they were delivered in 1936/7. They were the largest batch of motorbuses to enter service pre-war and also the last double-deckers. This rare, but admittedly sub-standard, view shows No. 153, RV 9307 in as delivered condition at the Red Lion, Cosham. Note the extremely large tramway style gilt fleet number and the use of the lower destination box to display 'Portsmouth Corporation'. It was the policy pre-war for this display to be shown in the lower box when operating normal services. Specials and extras displayed the destination in this box, with a white blank in the upper larger box.

Another of the large Craven-bodied order, No. 145, RV 9399 heads away from Cosham Railway Station en route to Highbury Estate. The old Cosham Compound site, abandoned in 1948, is on the left. *(ABC)*

Two of the Craven-bodied AECs, Nos 251 and 244, at the Dockyard in the early post-war period. The practice of showing 'Portsmouth Corporation' in the lower box was not reintroduced after the war and an ultimate destination was shown. Until new screens for the larger box arrived in 1948, the pre-war screens continued in use, which rather confusingly show a final destination as well. *(ADP)*

from October between Eastern Road and Edinburgh Road via Langstone Road and thence as the C-D. The year also saw the withdrawal of the last of the Karriers. The Coronation of 1937 gave the department the opportunity to continue a practice that had been prevalent in tram days, that of decorating an electric vehicle by way of celebration. Number 4 was the chosen vehicle and it was to appear on future occasions in similar guise, though by then renumbered 204. Although the pre-war network had been completed in November 1936, within a year it was necessary to suspend some services for no less than seven months with the result that around 25 trolleybuses were temporarily redundant. The services that were affected and which were temporarily motorbus operated were the 11-12 and 15-16, both of which travelled along New Road, where the removal of tram track had given rise to the need for the suspension of trolleybus operation. Electric operation re-commenced with effect from 31st May 1938 although tram track removal now commenced in Lake Road! It was apparently decided at this time that in future such work would be carried out in two parts so that trolleybus operation could be maintained. Whether in fact, largely in view of the incidence of the war, this policy was actually applied is open to conjecture. Indeed, right up to the final day of trolleybus operation roads were still being used with setts in

place and the tram track merely covered with tar. In fairness, this probably reflected the difference between the cost of lifting the rails and reinstating the roadway against the value of the metal rails.

In April 1939 a plot of land at the Alexandra Park end of Gladys Avenue which had been acquired by the Corporation some four years previously was cleared in preparation for the construction of a bus park which came into use the next month and which eliminated the requirement for buses on K-L and E-F to reverse at this point. At this stage it was not wired for trolleybus operation. Trolleybus No. 232 was fitted with trolley shoes in 1939 in place of trolley wheels and the rest of the fleet was subsequently changed. The final motorbuses to be delivered before the outbreak of hostilities arrived in the summer of 1939 and were six Leyland Cheetah saloons numbered 41-6 with quite attractive Wadham bodies fitted with sunshine roofs for use on the seafront service and intended to replace the time-expired Guys. They were briefly used on services M-N.

The final buses to be delivered in 1939 before the outbreak of war were five Wadham-bodied Leyland LZ4 single-deckers, intended principally for use on the seafront service. Two of them were blitz victims after only two years service and the final one, No. 46, BTP 946 is seen in Gladys Avenue outside North End depot. *(RM)*

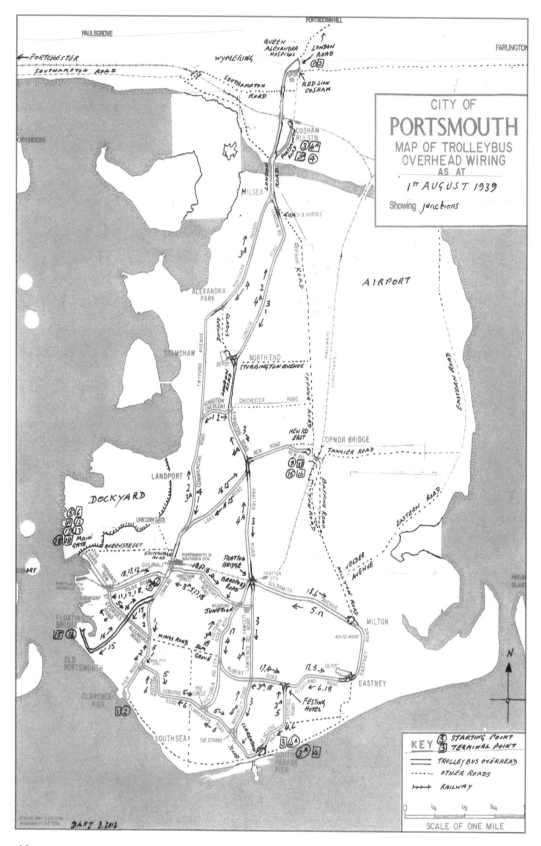

CITY OF
PORTSMOUTH
MAP OF TROLLEYBUS
OVERHEAD WIRING
AS AT
1st AUGUST 1939
Showing junctions

KEY S STARTING POINT
     T TERMINAL POINT
     TROLLEYBUS OVERHEAD
     OTHER ROADS
     RAILWAY

SCALE OF ONE MILE

40

Portsmouth's first trolleybus, No. 201, an English Electric-bodied AEC, was to remain in service until October 1958, following which it was purchased by the Ratepayers Association in 1960 and subsequently put on display at The Montague Motor Museum, later returning to the City under the care of the City's Museum Department.

The junction of Broad Street and East Street, in Old Portsmouth, (referred to as Floating Bridge on bus blinds) was the only place pre-war where trolleybuses in Portsmouth could be found carrying out a reversing manoeuvre. AEC/Craven No. 231 waits to depart on the original service 16 to Copnor Bridge which was introduced on 1st November 1936. This bus has a non-standard towing panel with four rows of louvres.

4 – The Second World War

Probably no other City in the country found itself in the situation that Portsmouth did at the outbreak of the Second World War and consequently it suffered quite substantially during the hostilities. Placed on the south coast, in itself an obvious target for invasion, it meant that approaching enemy aircraft could do so over water rather than over land and with the obvious prime target of the naval base located in the harbour, with numerous other military establishments close by, it was clearly a prime objective. Furthermore, it should not be forgotten that Portsmouth was built on an island, with extremely limited road and rail access. One of the first tasks facing the Transport Department was the evacuation of a large proportion of the population, which involved a substantial proportion of the motorbus fleet, to the obvious detriment of a number of services. After the war the population never regained the same level as it was prior to the evacuation.

The wartime brought modifications to the livery of nearly all bus fleets; in Portsmouth it resulted in the attractive white roofs being painted grey and it was not until 1960 that the pre-war style was restored. White lining out of mudguards, life-rails and platform edges was applied, as in most places, as an aid to recognition during the blackout. Later paint shortages resulted in overall khaki appearing and then grey with red bands. Destination blinds, not only in Portsmouth, were felt to be a considerable help to enemy spies, so along with the removal of road signs these too were modified. In particular 'DOCKYARD' was eliminated, despite the fact this was probably the busiest destination during the war! In addition the ultimate destination screen box ceased to show the 'PORTSMOUTH CORPORATION' display. This was in compliance with a Ministry instruction that required place names associated with Government establishments not to be shown; as part of this change motorbuses on C-D did not show City Airport either.

To replace the staff called-up, nearly 600 women were recruited; they included 490 platform staff among whom was, in 1940, the first woman in the country to qualify to drive both single- and double-deck buses. To save fuel many motorbus services were reduced together with the elimination of many stopping places and those areas which could be served by trolleybus saw motorbuses withdrawn, both services I-J and K-L being significantly reduced. A development that was not confined to Portsmouth but which had the same object, namely the reduction in fuel, saw a small number of the1931/2 Leyland Titan TD1s being used with gas producer trailers. The Government target was 10% of the fleet to be converted but this was rarely achieved. A further deterioration in the conflict resulted in the beach vicinities being declared prohibited areas and thus routes serving the seafront were reduced or diverted. This saw services 1-2, 3-4A, 3A-4, 5-6 and A-B affected.

The blitz caused much damage to the city and one of the worst raids occurred on 10th January 1941 when the Guildhall was burnt out and Clarence Pier destroyed. Two months later, on 10th March, nine buses and a former bus in use as an ancillary vehicle were destroyed at Eastney and many others damaged. The losses included two of the new Leyland Cheetahs and the sole AEC Regent. While these were the only actual victims during the war, at some time almost all vehicles received some damage which had to be dealt with by the department. Needless to say, at various times much overhead was also damaged, but generally it was able to be repaired so that by the time the affected road could be re-opened to traffic, trolleybuses were able to run once more.

In April 1941 the Municipal Passenger Transport Association (MPTA) was concerned about the practice relating to the publication of the trading results of Council trading Departments, which, in the case of Transport undertakings, not only covered the annual results, but also the periodic traffic returns, and wrote to the local authorities expressing concern. The Trade press certainly carried frequent articles comparing the differing results from the various Municipal undertakings. The MPTA was concerned that such returns could indicate the success of air raids and for reasons that are not now particularly clear it instanced the situation in Portsmouth. Some Town Clerks confirmed that Departments had a legal duty to publish information, but how the situation was resolved in Portsmouth, or indeed why it was felt appropriate to single the City out, will probably now never be known.

The reduction in demand resulted in surplus vehicles being loaned to other operators and the TSM double-deckers and some of the 1931 Titans were lent to London Transport, three of them subsequently being hired to Southampton Corporation. The four three-axle trolleybuses, which Nottingham had offered to buy in 1940, were lent to Pontypridd UDC in 1942. Southampton Corporation and Hants & Sussex Motor Services also received loans from the Corporation. The remainder of the trolleybuses numbered 201-24 had in fact been stored throughout the war as they were not fitted with traction batteries, unlike the rest of the fleet, and were considered a liability as they were rendered immobile when the overhead was damaged. These trolleybuses were stored on spare ground along Northern Parade and a TD1 always arrived at night with a crew in order to tow the vehicles away in the event of a fire following an air raid. The ability to manoeuvre trolleybuses short distances when power was cut off was obviously a benefit to any operator suffering the ravages of war.

Tom Dethridge, in his article on the undertaking published in *Buses Illustrated* in October 1964, summarised the service alterations during the war as follows:-

'Route changes included the complete suspension of summer holiday services such as G-H (Bransbury Road – Hayling Ferry), M-N and the seafront service. A-B was withdrawn in June 1942 between Palmerston Road and Cosham via the Guildhall; I-J was cut eventually to the section North End – Green Lane; an extension to Hilsea Halt in the winter of 1943 being very short-lived, lasting from 8th November

to December. K-L was reduced to a section Hayling Avenue to Bradford Junction and on 5th October 1941 was cut even more severely to Copnor Bridge only. The Highbury service was considerably reduced in frequency but subsequently on 31st May 1943 was extended to provide a link between Cosham and the new housing estates at Wymering. Service E-F remained though without the summer extension to Ferry Road but C-D was expanded on 17th July 1941 via the new Eastern Road and Eastern Road bridge (over Portscreek) to Farlington, Rectory Avenue. Of the trolleybus services, 1-2 to Clarence Pier was diverted to Osborne Road and then extended back to North End to remedy the loss of the I-J buses, while a new 1A-2A replaced the withdrawn section of the A-B and was then extended from Palmerston Road to Eastney shortly after and then to Milton where turning facilities existed. Service 3-4 was split in two from 21st July 1940, 3-4A running Cosham to Strand thence to the Dockyard while 3A-4 ran from Cosham to Albert Road as previously and then on to Eastney, Milton and Guildhall; these amended services made up for the withdrawal of the 5-6. Services 11-12 and 17-18 continued unaltered but the 15-16 was withdrawn at one period following the blocking of the road between Guildhall and Floating Bridge, this section being covered by a shuttle service of single-deck buses.'

One alteration to the trolleybus overhead that had been planned before the war and which it was possible to implement involved the introduction of wiring between Northern Road and Cosham compound via a private road, thus allowing

The first bus to be delivered during the war was No. 161, CTP 3, a Bedford OWB with a Duple 32-seat body. It arrived painted in an all-over brown livery but is seen here parked at Eastney depot in the final form of livery it carried. Note the carrier for the spare wheel.

43

During the war a number of vehicles were loaned to other operators to help meet their increased requirements and these included some of the 1932 TSMs. Some went to London Transport in 1940 and 1941 and also to Southampton Corporation in 1943 and 1944. The final loans were to the Hants & Sussex company in 1945/6 and No. 82, RV 1145, is seen here on such duty.

service 1 to serve Cosham Railway Station. The southbound overhead in Northern Road, although never again used for scheduled services, remained available and was used occasionally.

Acquisition of new buses during the war was not easy, it being necessary to convince both the Ministry of Supply and Ministry of War Transport of the need, but the losses mentioned above helped Portsmouth to be allocated ten single-deckers and nine double-deckers which entered service between 1942 and 1944. The single-deckers were a slightly unusual choice for a large municipal operator, albeit that it was the only war-time constructed chassis available, in the shape of Bedford's OWB model.

The first arrived in 1942 with a Duple body, followed a year later by two with Mulliner bodies and five with Duple bodywork, the final pair, also with Duple bodies, coming in 1944. All were delivered with 32 wooden slatted seats and received a dark brown unlined livery and one has

survived into preservation albeit with a replica body. Duple bodywork was also fitted to the double-deckers which arrived in 1944 and which had Daimler CW chassis fitted with AEC engines and were painted in a grey livery with a red band. All of these buses had bodywork built to the then austerity styles which were, of course, subject to the circumstances appertaining at the time.

Preparations for D-Day (6th June 1944) again gave rise to restrictions allowing access to the seafront area and a request was received from the War Department to dismantle the overhead leading to Clarence Pier. At the same time the 15-16 was again suspended for a period.

After D-Day these restrictions were lifted and trolleybus services resumed serving these termini. Before the end of 1944 it was found possible to introduce a new service G-H which replaced the remnants of the pre-war I-J and K-L, which operated from Green Lane via North End and New Road to Eastern Road.

The second wartime delivery, No. 162, CTP 19 another Bedford OWB, was fitted with Mulliner bodywork. It is seen at the Floating Bridge terminus of the 145 service, which operated as a shuttle to Guildhall on Sunday mornings.

After the war, initially the only buses in the fleet which could be operated with a driver only were the Bedfords and when, in January 1958, service 22 was introduced as a one-man-operated service they were the only option. Number 170, a Duple-bodied example, is seen at the Wymering Parr Road terminus.

The only double-deckers to be delivered during the war were nine Daimler CWA6s, also with Duple bodies. This rear view of No. 173, CTP 167, clearly shows the angular lines of the roof of a Utility body. *(ABC)*

Operating on a local service K at Cosham Railway Station is No. 176, CTP 177, still with its original body by Duple. *(RM)*

5 – Peace returns

On 13th May 1945, within a week of VE-day being celebrated (8th May), it was possible to restore some of the cuts and diversions that had been made. These included A-B and 3-4A and the re-introduction of 5-6, although it was in a shortened form, running between the Dockyard and the White House at Milton via South Parade Pier only. An indication of the move to the return of normality saw trolleybus No. 204 again running as an illuminated vehicle in May 1945. Trolleybus services returned to Clarence Pier from 29th July that year when the 1-2 was diverted to serve this point. From the same day an un-numbered service was introduced from Clarence Pier to Copnor Bridge via Strand and Fratton Bridge. Before the end of the year the remaining two three-axle trolleybuses which had been loaned to Pontypridd returned, the other pair having come home in March 1945.

The long running question of co-ordination between the two major transport operators in Portsmouth was to occupy quite a period of time over the next few months, the subject of which had been raised by no less an authority than the Regional Traffic Commissioner, who was responsible for, among other matters, the licensing of services and the level of fares. Like other issues in Portsmouth, it was to involve a public referendum but the consequence was that from 1st July 1946 a new agreement became effective. It covered an area bounded by Fareham, Petersfield and Emsworth within which Portsmouth Corporation was to operate 57% of the mileage and Southdown Motor Services 43%, the revenue to be shared on a similar basis. Like all such agreements involving a local authority it required an Act of Parliament but this also included provision for the company to operate trolleybuses. Since it provided that the balance of any mileage deficit in a given year should be restored by hiring bus(es) from the other party, this led to the use, at various times, of Southdown Guys or Leylands on the E-F, J-K, 3-4, 145 and 148 with Corporation buses operating on Southdown routes at other times. The Bedford OWBs were even used in this connection; a severe weight restriction on Langstone Harbour bridge for many years gave Southdown difficulties in finding suitable light-weight buses to operate the 47 service to Hayling

Island and the Bedfords were ideal for this when mileage balancing was necessary. They were also known to have worked on service 67, Havant and Compton. The joint agreement was to run for 21 years and was in fact renewed in June 1967 for a further ten, although the opportunity was taken to replace the rather unusual mileage balancing with a cash settlement at this time.

The same date of 1st July 1946 also saw the introduction of the summer timetable which was accompanied by a number of service changes. Service 1-2 (Cosham – Clarence Pier) was re-instated while the un-numbered service which had been running to Clarence Pier became the 7-8. Two other new trolleybus services were introduced; these were the 9-10 (Cosham, Red Lion-Guildhall - Victoria Road - Cosham) and the 13-14 (Cosham - Victoria Road - South Parade Pier). A turning circle at Alexandra Park also came into use for journeys on the 3A-4. When the 15-16 was re-instated on 29th September there were 11 trolleybus services in operation, the most during the whole of the time they were in use. At the same time the 1-2 was diverted to the Dockyard in lieu of Clarence Pier, but this arrangement was to be short-lived as from May 1947 it was replaced by the M-N motorbus service, which was extended to Farlington, a visible sign of the first fruits of the co-ordination agreement. Despite this apparent move towards trolleybus abandonment, the 1947/8 session of Parliament saw trolleybus operating powers being sought for a number of extensions, which included those for Farlington and Paulsgrove. The latter had been served since 18th May 1947 by an extended A-B. Among the buses withdrawn this year was the original Crossley Condor, No. 74. It was subsequently rebuilt by the department as a breakdown lorry and lasted in this form until 1971 since when it has been preserved and is probably the only complete and working Condor in existence.

The final new trolleybus service numbers to appear in the city did so on 26th September 1948 when the 19-20 was introduced as the opportunity was taken to eliminate route numbers with suffix letters. Thus the 1A, 2A, 3A and 4A became the 1, 2, 20 and 4, the existing 4 becoming 19. The 'new' services 3-4 and 19-20, which all terminated at Cosham Railway Station, were able to use the new layout at the compound which had come into use the previous month. The end of 1947 saw the introduction of the first post-war motorbuses. It was to be some time before production could return to pre-war levels but the department had ordered 25 of its new post-war chassis from Leyland as soon as circumstances permitted. Before any of these new buses had arrived, a further order was placed with Crossley for 31 DD42 models. These orders included the introduction of a new body-builder to the fleet, the local firm of Reading & Co Ltd, who were situated on London Road at Hilsea. Indeed, the first of the post-war buses, two Leyland PD1As, received bodywork by Reading. In 1948 ten more Reading bodies were delivered, on chassis split equally between Leyland and Crossley. The largest order for 1948 was for 19 Leyland PD1/PD1As with Weymann bodies. The PD1 and PD1A were virtually identical, the only difference being to the road spring attachments where the latter had Metalastik rubber bushes on the shackle pins rather than the metal bushes on the former. Two more Crossleys with Reading bodies arrived the next year, this combination being unique to Portsmouth, but the balance of the order carried Crossley's own bodywork.

On 29th May 1949 M-N was further extended to Leigh Park, a large housing estate owned and being developed by the Corporation to the north of

Havant but some miles outside the City Boundary, exactly the circumstances in which the co-ordination agreement benefitted the Corporation. Leigh Park was not one of the destinations for which trolleybus powers had been sought and the following year, on 17th June 1950 service 1-2 (formerly 1A-2A) was replaced by new bus service R-S, which whilst similar to the A-B, ran to Portchester rather than Paulsgrove. Trolleybus powers had been obtained to Paulsgrove but the continuation of such operation was by no means a foregone conclusion at this time.

Nevertheless, a large proportion of the trolleybus fleet, which had borne the bulk of the heavy work during the war, was to undergo significant rebuilding, using Metal Sections fabrications, and most of the Craven-bodied AECs were dealt with between 1948 and 1956. The first two dozen vehicles which had been stored

The first post-war delivery, No. 199, DTP 808 arrived in November 1947 and was an example of Leyland's new chassis, designated PD1A and fitted with Leyland's 7.4 litre diesel engine which had been developed for use in tanks. The choice of bodybuilder broke new ground in that the local firm of Reading & Co, who were based in Hilsea, supplied it together with eleven more bodies in 1947/8. The location is the Guildhall.

In a carefully posed picture for the trade press which appeared in *Passenger Transport* in March 1946, No. 98 is seen with the General Manager, Ben Hall, and Major HD Stevens of Crossley Motors. The article related to the 'Fifteen Years' Hard Work' which had been performed by 'these veteran Crossley buses' and the fact that this particular bus had completed 337,872 miles at an average of 9.5 miles per gallon.

Cosham compound in 1947 before the smaller turning circle came into use in 1948. Prominent are motorbus No. 155, one of the large pre-war batch of Craven-bodied Leyland TD4s and trolleybus No. 209, RV 4657, the English Electric-bodied Karrier E4. *(ADP)*

Two Reading-bodied Leylands arrived in 1947; one of which, No. 200, DTP 809, is seen here at Clarence Pier.

In 1948 fleet numbering reverted to number 1, and this vehicle, DTP 810, a Leyland PD1, is seen at the Dockyard in July 1949 on service N, which had been extended to Leigh Park on 25th May that year. *(ABC)*

The final Reading-bodied Leyland was No. 4, DTP 813. South Parade Pier is the location.

Reading & Co also bodied six Crossley DD42/5Ts in 1948/9, a combination unique to Portsmouth Corporation and No. 15, EBK 27, is seen here on route 'P' at North End junction. *(STA)*

Yet another bodybuilder new to the Corporation appeared in 1948 when 19 Weymann-bodied Leylands entered service. The large fleet numbers displayed on the front of vehicles until 1957 are clearly seen in this view of No. 194, DRV 108 while operating on the S.

Later, Dockyard terminus of the 148A, which had been the M-N service prior to June 1955. *(ABC)*

Climbing up, such as it is, the slope on Northern Road at Cosham over the Southern Region line to Southampton, No. 184, DTP 818, has travelled from Portchester on service 145.

After the success of the pre-war Crossley Condors, it was no surprise that Crossleys were ordered after the war. Apart from the handful of Reading-bodied examples, 25 more carried Crossley's own bodywork. No.39, EBK 576, leaves the Dockyard for the final leg of service C to Eastney Road.

during the war had all, with the exception of No. 212, re-entered service following overhaul. New trolleybuses were on order and the first of these entered service on 1st November 1950. They were BUT 9611Ts (virtually a post-war version of the AEC 661T) built by the Kingston-based company British United Traction which was the organisation formed by the merger of AEC's and Leyland's trolleybus interests after the war.

The bodies on the BUT's were built by Burlingham, who were based in Blackpool and represented that company's first trolleybus bodies, although they were to receive subsequent orders for trolleybuses from Manchester, Glasgow and Reading. They were the last Portsmouth vehicles to be fitted with an off-side destination screen and also had an unusual pair of single seats in the centre of the lower saloon which marked them out from the Craven bodies (a similar arrangement was also found on the Crossley bodies). The final one of the batch of 15 entered service in March 1951 and it was during the delivery of these vehicles that the department saw a change in General Manager. Ben Hall had been in charge since 1926 and his replacement was HC Simmonds who had been his deputy.

The new General Manager's views on trolleybuses were perhaps not as enthusiastic as those of his predecessor, but work was already underway to introduce trolleybuses along

The only post-war trolleybuses delivered to Portsmouth arrived in 1950 and 1951 and were BUT 9611T models with Burlingham 52-seat bodywork; the first trolleybuses in the country to be built by them. Number 304, ERV 929 has just left the terminal point at South Parade Pier on its journey north to Cosham Railway Station on service 4, the original trolleybus route in the city. Note that the offside screen is in use, a practice which soon ceased. *(STA)*

roads which had been included in the 1948 Act. Principally, this involved Milton Road and Copnor Road but instead of using Stubbington Avenue, authorisation was obtained to use an alternative in Chichester Road. Against these extensions, the Floating Bridge section was abandoned at the end of September 1951 without, seemingly, significant advance notice. The section to the Guildhall which would otherwise have been uncovered was initially served by the diversion of Southdown service 39 but from 25th May 1952 the R-S was revised to run Portchester – Floating Bridge. This abandonment removed the only trolleybus reverser in use on the system at the time. From 6th January 1952 services 7-8 and 11-12 were extended from Copnor Bridge to Green Lane, where the terminal arrangements involved trolleybuses turning into Madeira Road and then reversing into Compton Road. Was the reversing equipment originally installed at Floating

AEC 661T with Craven body, No. 233, RV 8315, is almost at the limit of the overhead in Compton Road, having reversed out of Madeira Road at the Green Lane terminus of services 11-12, to which point services were extended in January 1952. *(ADP)*

Only alternate journeys on service 12 from the Dockyard operated as far as Green Lane after the Copnor Road section was opened for trolleybuses and here AEC No. 273, RV 9124, turns at Copnor Bridge with the correct destination display which incorporates '(only)' in the ultimate destination box. *(ADP)*

Number 306, ERV 931, stands at the Red Lion terminus at Cosham on service 6 which reached this point from May 1952. *(ADP)*

The location is the White House at Milton, where a complete turning circle was provided. Disappearing into the background is Milton Road, which was first used by trolleybuses on 25th May 1952. BUT No. 301, ERV 926, on service 6 completes the picture.

Bridge required for this location, one wonders? Timetable-wise, generally only alternate journeys on services 11-12 were extended from Copnor Bridge to Green Lane. The final part of the 1948 scheme in this area saw the 5-6 extended from the White House to Cosham via Milton Road and Copnor Road from 25th May 1952. This covered a section of the R-S which had been diverted to the Floating Bridge from the same date.

The last of the 1931/2 buses were withdrawn after a very respectable 20-year service life in 1952 to be replaced by 25 more Titans, this time the first PD2/10 models which were fitted with Leyland's own attractive bodywork, built at their Farington plant. They also introduced an intriguing feature of Portsmouth's buses whereby the final bus of the batch used the registration mark '999', preceding buses in the batch carrying appropriate consecutive numbers. This feature was to apply to deliveries of new buses for the next eight years, and was said to have occurred when an employee of the Council's motor tax department, with an obvious interest in public transport, ensured that this particular number was allocated to the final bus in each delivery. Thus fleet Nos. 58-82 carried GTP 975-99.

Coronation year 1953 brought a number of opportunities and developments in Portsmouth which included the introduction of open-top buses and a new trolleybus route. The Coronation took place on 2nd June and in connection with this a Naval Fleet Review took place off Spithead which brought an increase in visitors to the city. In connection with the Coronation, trolleybus No. 204 re-appeared as an illuminated vehicle and ran throughout the summer, although no passengers were carried on these trips. This was the last time it was used, but it was not officially withdrawn until 1955. This length of time between last use and official withdrawal of trolleybuses was not unusual. On the motorbus front, one of the 1935 English Electric-bodied Leyland TD4s, No. 115, was converted to open-top form for use on the seafront service. Numbers 117, 124 and 125 were similarly converted over the next two years. The four remaining Leyland Cheetahs had maintained this service up until then but were retired the following year. At the end of the summer the provision of overhead wiring along Chichester Road and Gladys Avenue together with alterations to the junctions at Eastney, Chichester Road/

Leyland's final bodywork was perhaps among the best looking produced by the company, and in 1952 Portsmouth took 25 PD2/10s with this combination. No. 63, GTP 980, is depicted in Tangier Road Copnor. Unusually, these bodies featured half-drop windows rather than the sliders normally fitted to this type of body by Leyland.

The first Leyland TD4 to be converted to open-top was No.115 in 1953 and is seen here leaving Clarence Pier still carrying its original fleet number.

In 1953 the Corporation commenced operating the 'out-of-town' services 37/37A to Waterlooville, as a result of the joint co-ordination agreement. All Leyland No. 76, GTP 993, waits at Clarence Pier on the 37A variation. *(STA)*

Standing in East Street, Old Portsmouth, the road into which the service 15-16 trolleybuses once reversed, No. 148, RV 9402 is working a Floating Bridge – Guildhall shuttle. *(RM)*

Copnor Road, North End and Alexandra Park were made in completion of the 1948 powers so that from 27th September a new 15-16 service could be introduced replacing the F-E. This increase in trolleybus mileage was balanced to an extent by the withdrawal of the 9-10 trolleybus service the previous day, due to a reduction in traffic. One interesting feature of the new arrangements was that service 16 had a completely separate set of wires from Gladys Avenue to Chichester Road. The introduction of the new overhead also resulted in trolleybuses terminating at Copnor Bridge in the evening, returning to North End depot via Copnor Road and Chichester Road, rather than returning via New Road and Kingston Road, the junction of which had never been provided with a right turn in the overhead, the turn always being made on battery. An interesting development occurred on 11th November 1954 when a new undesignated service linking Wymering and Hilsea Lido was introduced. It was allocated the route number 21 from 12th June 1955. This was a break with tradition from two aspects; firstly it was a numbered motorbus service and secondly the route number was used in both directions.

Like many wartime-built buses, the bodywork on the Daimlers was constructed using materials available at the time which were not necessarily those which would have been chosen in other circumstances. In Portsmouth's case the decision was taken to rebody these buses and they re-entered service in 1955 with new Crossley 56-

seat bodies. The same year saw an unusual visitor to Portsmouth in the shape of a Walsall Sunbeam F4A trolleybus which ran on services 5-6, and 19-20 during the Municipal Passenger Transport Association conference in September.

Reference has already been made the extension of services to Leigh Park, which lay outside the City and from June 1955 the M-N was renumbered 148A and 148B, depending on the outer terminus and was the first Corporation service to be numbered in the Southdown route number series. Not long after, on 25th September the second such service appeared when the R-S became the 145. Such was the demand for services to and from Leigh Park that from the end of September 1956 overnight parking of buses on the Estate commenced, with the majority of crews living locally who had the use of one of the Bedford OWBs for crew facilities. That same year, 1956, also saw the entry into service of 25 Leyland PD2/12s but this time there was a new bodybuilder, for Leyland had closed their bodywork department and Metro-Cammell provided the bodies from their Birmingham factory. At that time orders for Leyland chassis would often be fitted with MCW group bodywork whilst AECs would be bodied by Park Royal.

The next few years were overshadowed by a lengthy public debate concerning the future of the trolleybus system. We have already seen that issues affecting public transport in the city had often been subject to considerable discussion and

59

In 1959 the Daimlers were sent to Stockport to receive new, attractive four-bay bodies. Number 173 is seen at the 145 terminus at Old Portsmouth ready to leave for Portchester. **(ABC)**

Pulling away from the foot of the Guildhall steps, No. 178, now fitted with its new body by Crossley, is operating on service B.

An off-side view of No. 177 at South Parade Pier after repainting with a white roof (a variation to the fleet livery re-introduced in 1960) and the fitment of flashing indicators.

In September 1955 the rather unusual sight of a 'foreign' trolleybus operating in Portsmouth could be seen, when Walsall 864 was used on several services during the MPTA conference in the city. It was a Sunbeam F4A with Willowbrook 70-seat body, a significantly higher capacity than anything else in the fleet at the time.

In 1956 Portsmouth turned to Metro-Cammell as the supplier of its bus bodies for double-deckers and this was to remain the case for the next ten years. Twenty five Leyland PD2/12s were involved in this order. With two Isle of Wight paddle steamers in the background, No. 97, LRV 989, waits on the 148B stand at the Dockyard. The suffix letter of the route number indicated the route and terminus in Leigh Park. Note the provision still of a semaphore arm for signalling. Returning from that location is another Leyland PD2/12, number 104, this time operating on service 148A and seen at Bedhampton.

even referenda but seldom can an operator been faced with such a sustained opposition over policy. Greater Portsmouth was blessed with no less than four Ratepayers Associations and they, together with the Trades Council, mounted an extremely vocal campaign to retain the trolleybuses, assisted in no small way by an accommodating local press.

The Transport Committee decided in July 1956 to gradually replace trolleybuses with motor buses and the City Council had confirmed this decision in October. But the Suez crisis and the fuel rationing that followed put the operation of trolleybuses in a different light and in January 1957 the City Council voted to reconsider the plans. Subsequently, a decision was taken in October 1958 to engage consultants to review the whole issue and they eventually reported back in September 1959, concluding that the abandonment policy was 'sound'. By this time the last of the 1934 trolleybuses (No. 201) had been withdrawn along with the last of the 1935 trolleybuses (No. 224). Number 201 was subsequently on display at Beaulieu Motor Museum for a number of years and more recently at the Milestones Museum in Basingstoke. It is currently stored at the City of Portsmouth Passenger Transport depot which is not open to the public.

Service 13-14, which had led a charmed existence for some years, being liable to augmentation, but more likely withdrawal without notice, finally succumbed on 24th January 1959. This created capacity problems between Cosham and Fratton Bridge on Saturdays and so from 14th February an undesignated service was introduced between these two points. As with a couple of late night journeys, and also previously 13-14, trolleybuses turned via Rigby Road and took their layover at the Bradford Junction end, where there was, for many years, the last cast iron pre-war bus stop in the City. The east-bound wiring in Rigby Road was never used by timetabled services, and there is no record of it having been used either in an emergency or for trolleybus tours.

On the motorbus front, the arrival of 15 Leyland PD2/40s (Nos. 108-22), the last of this model acquired, were delivered during 1958 and resulted in the four open-top TD4s receiving new fleet numbers 5-8 to make way for them. The only single-deck buses in the fleet gained something of a reprieve when service 22 (again a single number for the route) was introduced on 13th January 1958

between Upper Drayton and Cosham using the Bedford OWBs as one-person-operated vehicles. Modifications which permitted the driver to open the doors had been implemented. The service was extended in May to Wymering.

Reference has previously been made to the rebuilding of the AEC trolleybuses. One distinguishing feature on some of these trolleybuses was the replacement of the front upper deck half drop windows with fixed panes, although this alteration did not always coincide with the major rebuild. The pre-war Craven-bodied Leyland TD4s also required major rebuilding during their life-time and the Leyland-bodied examples also proved troublesome in their early days. Of the post-war motorbuses, problems of a different kind were experienced. The Crossleys were delivered with Salerni Turbotransmitters and Crossley engines but withdrawal of Leyland TD4s during the late 1950s enabled the Crossley-bodied vehicles to be fitted with TD4 engines, clutches and gearboxes from the withdrawn vehicles. This modification was designed to improve efficiency and reliability, as the Crossley engines were somewhat thirsty in terms of fuel consumption. The condition of the Reading bodywork did not justify similar work on the other Crossleys.

The final Leyland Titans to enter the fleet did so in 1959 when five of the PD3/6 model arrived (Nos. 123-7), still with Metro-Cammell bodywork but they were the first 30ft buses in the fleet, with seats for 64. A few years later their capacity was increased to 70, and an emergency window had to be fitted at the front off-side of the lower saloon to meet the then emergency exit regulations. The last of the 1933 Titans were withdrawn as a result and 1935 TD4 No. 127 was renumbered to 129 to avoid duplication. Also ordered in 1959 were ten Leyland Tiger Cubs with Weymann dual-door bodies, intended to be operated by a driver only. Originally delivered in September 1959 with maroon roofs, their over-long sabbatical while a national agreement was reached permitting their use resulted in this being painted white, a feature that was subsequently extended to the whole of the motorbus fleet. Their delay in entering service did not escape the notice of the opposition party on the Council, nor one of the Ratepayers Associations, the attention of both serving to provide several more column inches in the local press.

A further order for 15 Leyland Titans, this time of the PD2/40 variety, was delivered in 1958 and No.114, ORV 991, is seen shortly after delivery. These were the first vehicles to be delivered with the smaller fleet number on the front.

In original livery and before the fitting of flashing indicators, Leyland PD2 N0. 113, ORV 990, passes through a rather quiet North End and past one of the most iconic shop fronts of the period.

English Electric-bodied Leyland TD4 No. 115, RV 6358, was the first of 12 similar buses delivered in 1935 and was the first to be converted to open-top in 1953. Five years after conversion it was renumbered 5. *(STA)*

The nearside view of the same vehicle taken at South Parade Pier shows that on the nearside it was possible to locate the City Crest in the correct position whereas on the offside it needed to be offset to clear the filler cap.

On 13th January 1958 service 22 was introduced as a one-man-operated service between Upper Drayton and Cosham Railway Station, being extended to Wymering on 18th May that year. From the start the wartime Bedfords were used and the penultimate one, Nos. 169, bodied by Duple, is seen at the Northern Road roundabout in Cosham en route to Drayton. The screen has not been changed for this journey!

After removal of the troublesome Crossley engines and their replacement with pre-war Leyland units, the Crossleys were frequently to be found on the 19-20. No. 48, EBK 581, passes under Portsmouth & Southsea Station railway bridge on the service 19 leg to Alexandra Park. The group of sailors would be a regular sight in the streets at the time.

After receiving the same Leyland engine conversion, No. 50, EBK 583, is seen on Portsbridge on service 19 to Eastney.

As was often the case with pre-delivery manufacturer's official photographs, in this case commissioned by Metro-Cammell, incorrect blinds have been fitted to No. 124, STP 996. The blind in the upper box should be in the lower one and vice versa. Photographed on Southsea Common, ASRE. was one of Portsmouth's more mysterious displays, albeit connected with the Royal Navy, which was not unusual in Portsmouth. ASRE stood for Admiralty Signal and Radar Establishment, which later became Admiralty Surface Weapons Establishment (ASWE), which was located at the top of Portsdown Hill, east of Fort Southwick, and recently demolished. Special stage carriage services were operated. *(STA)*

The last open platform buses arrived in Portsmouth in 1959 – five Leyland PD3/6 models which were the first 30ft double-deckers in the fleet. Number 123, STP 995, arrives at the Dockyard from Farlington.

Now with white roof and small white fleet number, Leyland PD3 No. 125, STP 997, heads through Southsea on service 1. Note the second window from the front on the lower-deck which has been fitted with an emergency exit as a result of the seating capacity being increased from 64 to 70 in 1972.

The rebuilding of Nos. 127 and 128 in 1957 involved the alteration of the front destination boxes to the later style. The arrival of the Leyland PD3s in 1959 and the fortuitous withdrawal of the original No. 129 resulted in No. 127 being renumbered 129 that year. Nos. 128 and (new) 129 are seen in Eastney depot. *(PT)*

A rear view of the renumbered 129 turning into Western Esplanade on a Private Hire, which seem to be carrying Naval WRNS in Portsmouth.

A study of Leyland bodywork 'before and after' from a less conventional angle, with a rear view of No.130 in original condition. As delivered, this bus had a torque convertor but was fitted with a conventional Leyland TD4 gearbox in 1947. The picture was taken awaiting the Dockyard outmuster. *(DAPJ)*

Number 128 after rebuilding of the Leyland bodywork in 1957 by the Corporation, particular attention having been paid to the destination displays. This batch of buses had all-metal construction, among the first so built by Leyland. The innovation was not without problems in the early days. This picture was taken at South Parade Pier. *(DAPJ)*

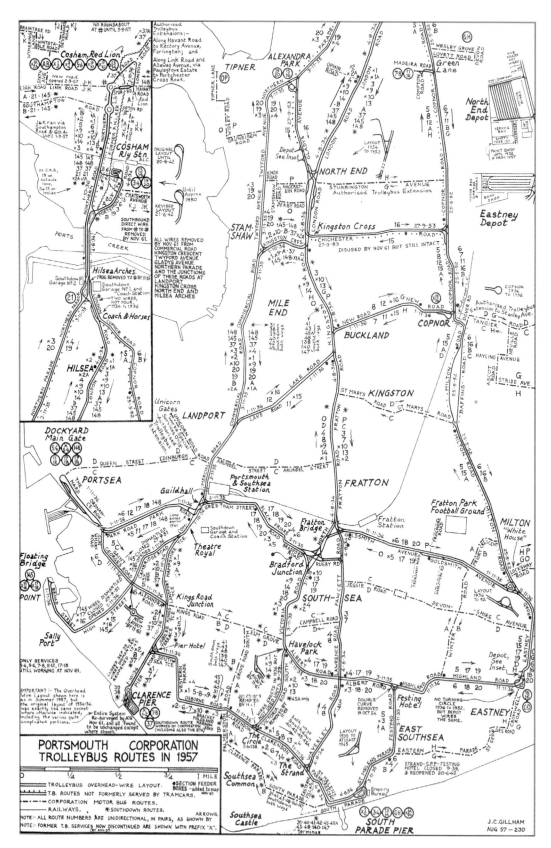

PORTSMOUTH CORPORATION TROLLEYBUS ROUTES IN 1957

TROLLEYBUS OVERHEAD-WIRE LAYOUT.   #SECTION FEEDER BOXES - added to map Nov 61.
T.B. ROUTES NOT FORMERLY SERVED BY TRAMCARS.
CORPORATION MOTOR BUS ROUTES.
RAILWAYS.   *SOUTHDOWN ROUTES.
NOTE:- ALL ROUTE NUMBERS ARE UNIDIRECTIONAL, IN PAIRS, AS SHOWN BY ARROWS.
NOTE:- FORMER T.B. SERVICES NOW DISCONTINUED ARE SHOWN WITH PREFIX "X".

J.C.GILLHAM
AUG 57 - 230

The desire to eliminate suffix letters on the Corporation's services led to the introduction of the 19-20 in September 1948, as described in the text and this was the highest numbered trolleybus service. AEC No. 233 heads for Alexandra Park. Numbers 243 and 240, below, provide a classic view of the post-war trolleybus scene in Portsmouth at probably the most photographed location.

Trolleybus
Twilight

In September 1959 the decision by the Transport Department to abandon the use of trolleybuses was finally confirmed. Over the next few pages there follows a very brief review of the final years of the last trolleybus services.

Craven-bodied No. 233, RV 8315, is seen, top, at the service 3 starting point at Cosham Railway Station before setting off for South Parade Pier. *(ADP)*

At the terminal of service 3 (and the starting point for service 4) seen centre, is No. 283, RV 9134, laying-over on the private road at South Parade Pier. It is July 1959 and the service has but 14 months of trolleybus operation remaining. *(ADP)*

Crossing the Southern Region electrified line out of Portsmouth at Copnor Bridge, No. 307, ERV 932, having left the Dockyard with the destination display 'South Parade Pier', now displays the ultimate destination of service 5. *(ADP)*

BUT No. 302, ERV 927, heads a line of vehicles at the Red Lion, Cosham, the 5-6 terminus. The AEC behind is No. 274 on a Southern Counties Touring Society tour on 4th June 1963. It was almost certainly the last vehicle to use the passing loop which was removed two months later. One of the Leyland PD3s operating to the Dockyard on service 148A/148B is at the rear. *(ADP)*

Highbury Buildings on Portsmouth Road, Cosham, a classic 1930s style shopping and residential block, form the background to No. 255, RV 9106, heading for Southsea on service 6. Note that although this vehicle carries semaphore traffic arms the driver is wisely using hand signals.*(ADP)*

Having just passed under the overhead junction leading to the terminus of services 7-8 and 11-12, No. 308, ERV 933, will head up Copnor Road towards Eastney on service 6. At Milton the display 'Palmerston Road' will be changed to 'Dockyard'.*(ADP)*

75

BUT No. 314, ERV 939, has just turned off Southsea seafront into Clarendon Road on service 6. *(ADP)*

The terminus for service 11-12 was in Madeira Road, although always called 'Green Lane' on the destination blinds. With only six months of the service left, No 273, RV 9124, has just turned right into Copnor Road from the terminal point for services 11-12 at Green Lane. *(ADP)*

Cosham Railway Station was also the northern terminus of the 13-14, the use of Victoria Road in Southsea distinguishing it from the 3-4.

An apparently deserted Guildhall Square gives AEC No. 283, RV 9134, easy negotiation across this normally busy junction on service 17. This bus was one of eight similar trolleybuses which lasted until the penultimate month of operation. David Packer captured the scene on 7th April 1963. *(ADP)*

At the other end of Greetham Street No. 283, RV 9134, leaves the cobbles and prepares to turn into Blackfriars Road. All of this area has now been redeveloped. *(ADP)*

Service 17 forked right at Bradford Junction en route to Eastney and No. 286, RV 9137, approaches the unusual triangular shaped shelter at this point. *(ADP)*

Later in the same day as the picture at the top of the previous page it would appear that rain has now moved in from the channel as No. 274, RV 9125, on service 18, approaches the loading point in Greetham Street. *(ADP)*

Post-war BUT No. 304, ERV 929, speeds across the northern leg of Bradford Junction in April 1963. By this time the wiring into Rugby Road from Bradford Road has been removed. The ears where running wire has been spliced in may be seen. *(ADP)*

Next door to the Gaumont Cinema at Bradford Junction was the Emmanuel Baptist Church, being passed by No. 304, ERV 929, on its way back to the Dockyard. *(ADP)*

A final view at Cosham Railway Station as 1937 AEC/Craven No. 297, RV 9151, is about to set off on the first leg of a journey on service 19 which would eventually terminate at Alexandra Park. *(ADP)*

The lower deck interior of the Craven-bodied AECs was extremely comfortable with typical 1930s décor. *(RGR)*

Outside the Highland Road entrance to Eastney depot was the location of the terminus of service 15-16, where BUT No. 304 waits to depart on the 18-minute journey to Alexandra Park.

PORTSMOUTH BUS POLICY VINDICATED

"Sound" Move To Abandon Trolly System

PORTSMOUTH City Council's policy over trolly buses and the co-ordination agreement with Southdown Motor Services Ltd. has been vindicated.

Findings of the consultants appointed to conduct an inquiry into these issues were accepted at a special meeting of the Passenger Transport Committee today lasting 20 minutes.

These described the policy of the abandonment of trolly buses in the City and the joint co-ordination area during the next 20 years to be sound, and the agreement to be satisfactory.

After receiving the 32-page report of the consultants, Harold Whitehead and Partners Ltd., the Committee passed a recommendation that the report of the General Manager and Engineer (Mr. H. Simmonds) concerning the first stage implementation of the handomment policy, should be put into effect.

If the City Council passes this at its next meeting, it will mean that services 3/4 (Cosham to South Parade Pier via London Road, Fratton Road, and Fawcett Road), 13/14 (via London Road, Fratton Road, and Victoria Road), and 7/8 (Green Lane to Clarence Pier), will be withdrawn.

The committee also recommends that Mr. Simmonds should be instructed to submit for consideration further plans for the withdrawal or substitution of trolly buses, as circumstances of vehicle decision and traffic requirements develop.

When Ald. S. R. Thorrowgood asked the committee chairman (Alderman H. E. Collins) if he was "happy" at the report, the chairman replied: "I have been happy all along, but not with the procrastination and the controversy which has been brought along so unnecessarily."

Alderman A. Johnson asked, "Will the General Manager say whether the report contains any revelations to him?"

"Waste" Claim

And when Mr. Simmonds gave a negative reply, Alderman Johnson added: "Then it has been a waste of money."

The cost of this first stage of the consultants' report was stated to be £2,520.

Earlier, Councillor M. J. E. Wallis had asked, "As this has been one of the most controversial subjects in Portsmouth for years, will everyone be satisfied that the report represents money well spent?"

The chairman replied: "That is a matter of opinion. It came about as a resolution of this committee due to circumstances well known to yourself.

"And it was also verbally agreed that every member of the council, including the opposition, would stand by the report when it was produced."

Second part

A second part of the assignment related to setting up a system of cost control through standards at a further estimated fee of £2,520. It is understood that work on the second stage is now proceeding, and will be the subject of a further report on September 15.

After concluding that the abandonment of trolly buses decision was sound, the report of the consultants continued:

"By so doing, a flexibility will be achieved which will enable the services and the routing to be adapted readily to changing demands.

"At the end of the period (20 years or so) a new situation will have evolved when it might be expedient to reconsider the whole matter.

"In our view it is likely that by that time, new means of propulsion will be available without the respective disadvantages of both diesel buses and trolly buses."

Concerning co-ordination, the report stated that a form of agreement covering the whole area was necessary.

Satisfactory

The consultants added: "The present agreement is a satisfactory one and should be continued. We would not seek to change any material aspect of it.

"Under Clause 4 of the Portsmouth Corporation Act, 1946, the two parties are given wide freedom to make such modification of the terms as may at any time be agreed between them.

"Consequently it will not be necessary to draft an entirely new agreement to enable the co-ordination to be adapted to new circumstances."

During the inquiry, the consultants stated, they had access to all Corporation records, willing co-operation of officers and other interested bodies, and discussions with the Joint Committee of local ratepayers' associations, Portsmouth Trades Council, Portsmouth Chamber of Commerce, and among others, with the transport managers of nine other municipalities.

(Reasons for the findings are given in 30 pages of the report, and these will be summarized in tomorrow's Evening News.).

GREEN LIGHT AT LAST FOR TEN IDLE BUSES

Starting Date is April 3

PORTSMOUTH'S ten one-man operated, single-deck buses, which have stood idle in the Passenger Transport Depots for some months, are to come into operation on Sunday, April 3.

This was stated by the Deputy Manager (Mr. A. W. Fielder), who added that they would begin operation on the J—K (Highbury Estate to Wymering Estate) and No. 21 (Hilsea Lido to Paulsgrove) services.

"The men who will man the buses are now undergoing training," he said. "They are all drivers, though most of them have had conducting experience."

It was in January last year that the Passenger Transport Committee decided to buy the ten buses, though the decision to take them into use was made at the City Council meeting in September, 1958.

Nine of the buses had been received by the beginning of October, 1959, though it was then stated that certain modifications were being made by the makers.

But because of national wage negotiations, the buses could not be put into service. At a meeting of the Passenger Transport Committee in January, the Chairman (Ald. H. E. Collins) was closely questioned about the delay in getting the buses into service.

At the next month's meeting of the Committee, the question of the "idle ten" was again raised, but this time, after some exchanges between Ald. S. R. Thorrowgood and Coun. C. H. Clark, the Committee went into private session to discuss the matter.

34 PASSENGERS

Each of the single-deck buses has cost £4,556. It will seat 34 passengers, with an additional authorised standing complement of six.

Mr. Fielder denied today that there had been any repainting of the buses as a result of their having to stand idle for five months.

"There has been some adjustment to the livery, to bring them in line with the rest of the transport fleet," he said.

One of Portsmouth's new single-deck buses.

The local press, in the form of the Portsmouth Evening News, followed the debate over the decision to close the trolleybus system (or 'trollybuses', as they always referred to them) and the subsequent one to introduce driver-only operated single-deckers very closely, as these extracts from issues in September 1959 and March 1960 show.

6 – The Sixties

The Leyland Tiger Cubs (Nos. 16-25) eventually entered service on 3rd April 1960 on services J-K and 21 and on the 1st May they also replaced the trolleybuses on 15-16, making this the shortest lived trolleybus route by far at just less than seven years. Other changes resulted in double-deck motorbuses replacing trolleybuses on the same day on the 19-20, which was extended to Paulsgrove. Generally this service utilised the re-invigorated Crossleys as rolling stock.

May saw the first double-decker (No. 200) out-shopped with a white roof, a welcome return to the pre-war motorbus style. The trolleybus repainting programme had by now ceased so this change was never applied to them. No redundant trolleybus overhead wiring had been removed at this stage with the result that when the Southern Counties Touring Society visited Portsmouth on Sunday 3rd July and used BUT No. 304 they were able to travel along Northern Parade and Chichester Road despite regular services having been withdrawn from them some two months before! The next trolleybus route to be replaced was the 3-4, which became motorbus operated from 18th September 1960 and which was also extended to Paulsgrove over the 21 route which was replaced. It was following this conversion that work commenced on removing the significant amount of trolleybus overhead that was still in place although no longer in use.

Further development of the Leigh Park services took place on 5th March 1961 when the C-D was extended to that location and renumbered 143 (or more accurately 143A-143F, depending on the terminus). All inbound journeys were just 143. For its deliveries that year the department at last realised that it was possible to request specific registration marks to coincide with the fleet number and so numbers 131-42 carried matching YBK marks. These too were single-deckers with Weymann dual-door bodies, but this time they were Leyland Leopards, not dissimilar from a Tiger Cub but with a larger engine. They entered service on 3rd December on the 7-8, the Green Lane terminus being moved to Devon Road and the G-H services, the latter being renumbered 9-10, with extensions to Eastney as 9A and the summer extension to South Parade Pier as 9B.

From the same day J-K became 23-24 and the 11-12 trolleybus route became motorbus operated as well. Journeys on this service terminating at Copnor Bridge were extended to Ebery Grove via Tangier Road. These changes meant that after 27 years North End depot no longer operated trolleybuses.

At the end of 1961 Portsmouth's first rear-engined double-deckers were ordered but delays in their delivery gave a brief reprieve for the final two trolleybus services. Originally intended to be bodied by Weymann's at Addlestone, these Leyland Atlanteans were in fact constructed by the other partner in the Metro-Cammell-Weymann organisation, Metropolitan Cammell Carriage & Wagon at their factory at Elmdon, Birmingham and it was not until the summer of 1963 that they arrived. A fire at the Weymann factory in July 1961 had led to the delay and had also resulted in Bournemouth Corporation losing a complete Sunbeam trolleybus which was in build. Seven more Leopards (Nos. 143-9) were also delivered in April/May 1963 to replace the remaining Bedfords which had an Indian Summer, as they were called upon to substitute for the newer o-m-o buses despite their lower seating capacity which tended to cause problems.

The 25 Atlanteans began arriving in May and after a period of driver familiarisation they initially entered service on the 143 and later on service 148. They were numbered 201-25 which was a break with tradition in that all vehicles numbered above 200 had hitherto been electric ones. These extra motorbuses in the fleet were to replace trolleybuses on the 17-18 from 23rd June and on the final trolleybus route, the 5-6, from 28th July. The last trolleybus to reach Eastney depot was No. 313, which has subsequently been preserved, and the actual last journey was along the 18 route from the Dockyard via Fratton Bridge and the White House at Milton, which although converted a month before, was still trolleybus operated for first and last journeys. Unlike the closure of the tram system, which was commemorated by the department, no such ceremonies of any sort marked the end of trolleybus operation, save that when No. 313 arrived at Eastney packed with enthusiasts, the writer included, the Deputy Manager, Mr A W Fielder, hung a floral wreath over the off-side mirror before it entered the depot. Although sold for scrap, 313 was subsequently

The 15-16 trolleybus service had barely six months to run when AEC No. 252 was captured on 3rd October 1959 at the Eastney terminus of this service, which was adjacent to Eastney depot, behind the photographer and to the right. *(DAPJ)*

Alexandra Park turning circle on Saturday 30th April 1960 – the last day of trolleybus operation of services 15-16 and 19-20. AEC No. 239 is on the latter while BUT 306 is on the former, whose display of 'Eastney (Only)' is a little odd, as service 16 in this form only ever went to Eastney! *(DAPJ)*

Although delivered in 1959, it would be the following year before Portsmouth's first underfloor single-deckers, Leyland Tiger Cubs bodied by Weymann, would enter service. Cosham local service J was one of the recipients of these buses and No. 16, TTP 990, has had its roof repainted white prior to entering traffic. They were the last batch to have the final vehicle in the order registered '999'. This view is at the Highbury Estate terminus. *(ABC)*

By the time this photo of No. 20, TTP 994, was taken the J-K had been renumbered 23-24 (from 3rd December 1961) and this nearside view of the Tiger Cub shows the addition external signs fitted for driver-only operation. It is turning into the Highbury Estate at Chatsworth Avenue. *(ABC)*

The entry into service of the first Leyland Leopards, also bodied by Weymann in December 1961, saw further extensions of one-man-operation. Their use saw G-H become 9-10 and the 7-8 trolleybuses replaced by these new single-deckers. In the upper view No. 133, YBK 133, stands at the South Parade Pier terminus of service 10 and in the lower picture No. 134, YBK 134, is at the Clarence Pier terminus of service 7. Information on the bus stop exhorts passengers to pay as they enter. *(ABC)*

The first service to be converted directly from trolleybus to one-man-operated single-deck operation was the 15-16 in April 1960. One of the 1961 Leyland Leopards is seen here in Eastney Road heading south; the screen has already been changed for the return journey on that service. *(ABC)*

A final delivery of Leyland Leopards arrived in 1963, ordered primarily as replacements for the Bedford OWBs. They comprised seven units and No. 148, 148 BTP, is at the Dockyard. This vehicle survives in preservation. *(ABC)*

Substituting for a Tiger Cub on 8th August 1960 found Bedford No. 161 on the J at Highbury Estate terminus. *(DAPJ)*

Capacity problems on Saturdays following the conversion to single-deck OMO buses of services 15-16 resulted in the Bedfords operating additional journeys to supplement the timetable. Bedford No. 163 is seen leaving North End depot in August 1962 before operating such a trip to Copnor Bridge. Note the '16 EXTRA' on the destination blind. *(DAPJ)*

Bedford No.165, also substituting for a single-deck Leyland, is seen operating along Fratton Road on service 7 (despite what the destination screen shows!) in March 1963, just weeks before its withdrawal. *(DAPJ)*

The same bus heads back to North End depot after another duty covering for one of the Leylands. *(FWY)*

The south coast is not well-known for bad winters but falls of snow do occur, as these two fine views by TV Runnacles demonstrate. In the upper picture an unidentified AEC returns to the Dockyard with an absence of other traffic, wisely avoiding the unpleasant driving conditions.

In the lower view a fellow AEC passes under the turning circle at Milton White House heading for Eastney, the destination blind has already been turned to Dockyard. In the distance a single-deck Leyland on service 15 heads towards Alexandra Park. The snow laden sky enhances the overhead in a way often lost in sunny weather. *(TVR both)*

No self-respecting trolleybus system would be without locations where unusual or infrequent manoeuvres took place. Towards the end of the system these sometimes over-looked antics tended to be given greater attention by the enthusiast. In the upper picture No.274, turns across Park Road, which ran at the side of the Guildhall.

The Southern Counties Touring Society's tour of Portsmouth in June 1963 utilising No. 274 has already been featured, but in this view it has now reached Southsea and is turning on the rarely used loop which had been erected in 1953 for the summer extension of service 15-16 from Eastney, which was never introduced. *(DAPJ both)*

Overtaking one of the rebodied Daimlers, which were withdrawn in 1965, Leyland Leopard No. 147, 147 BTP, passes through North End. *(ABC)*

One of the first Leyland Atlanteans, No. 207, 207 BTP, turns across the front of the Dockyard Main Gate (now Victory Gate) as it sets off for Cosham Red Lion on service 5. The screen has been incorrectly set for 'Paulsgrove' rather than 'Palmerston Road' which was presumably the adjacent display. *(ABC)*

The first rear-engined double-deckers arrived in 1963. This view of No. 212, 212 BTP, not only shows that rear destination displays were still used, but that no less than ten intermediate points are displayed.

Portsmouth's last trolleybus turns across Eastney Road to enter the depot for the last time on Saturday 27th July 1963. The trolleybus involved, No. 313, was subsequently rescued from the hands of a breaker and entered the realms of the preservationists and was operated in Bournemouth before that system closed and is now to be found at the East Anglian Transport Museum at Carlton Colville. *(RGF)*

rescued and in fact operated in Bournemouth in April 1967 before that system closed. It can now be found at the East Anglia Transport Museum at Carlton Colville where it has been fully restored.

The opportunity was taken at this time to eliminate the last of the lettered routes which for so long had been a feature of Portsmouth's operations, so that from 29th July the A-B became 1-2 and the O-P became 14-13. The seafront service, which had never shown a letter, became 25 and the other summer service, L, Bransbury Park (Eastney Road) to Hayling Ferry, became 26. The service 12 journeys which had been extended to Ebery Grove became 12B from the same date, the Green Lane ones becoming 12A. Before the end of the year another ten Leyland Atlanteans had entered service and a further ten arrived in 1964. Again, the intention had been for all these buses to be bodied by Weymann but they were in the end built in Birmingham, this time the delay in part being attributed to a 21-week strike at the Weymann factory.

This sizeable intake of new vehicles, besides, of course, replacing the last of the trolleybuses, also saw the last two pre-war motorbuses withdrawn, leaving just the open-top TD4s and a start was made taking the first of the post-war Leylands out of service, together with the Reading-bodied Crossley buses. The Daimlers were to follow soon after. The General Manager, Mr Simmonds, retired in 1965 and was succeeded by his Deputy, AW Fielder, who probably holds a unique position, not only at Portsmouth, but quite possibly within the municipal world as he rose from a tram conductor in 1924 to the most senior post in the same undertaking in 1965. He was to be followed as General Manager by his Traffic Superintendent, Mr R Palmer, in 1968. Regrettably, Mr Palmer held this position for less than year as a result of his untimely death and he in turn was succeeded by Mr RE Botterill.

Further Leyland Atlanteans entered service in 1966 but since the Weymann factory at Addlestone had by now been closed (ironically by Metro-Cammell itself) they had Met-Cam bodies. The emphasis on vehicle deliveries for the next five years was, however, specifically on those capable of being operated by one person, and at this time this meant single-deck buses. Thus 25 Leyland

Panther Cubs arrived in 1967 which resulted in the 5-6 and 17-18 becoming single-deck one-person-operated from 19th March and the 11/12/12A/12B and 13-14 being converted to single-deck one-person-operated from 13th November. The single-deck fleet was further increased by a dozen AEC Swifts in 1969 and a dozen Leyland Atlanteans, but with single-deck bodies, in 1971/2.

One of the results of these new buses entering service had been the withdrawal of all of the Crossleys and the 1952 Leylands whilst inroads had been made into the 1956 Leylands and a start of the withdrawal of even the Tiger Cubs. This rather mixed bag of new vehicles perhaps vividly illustrates the issues that many operators were struggling with at this time. The early rear-engined double-deckers were not in any case as reliable as the buses they replaced but they did have a lower step entrance when compared with the traditional underfloor single-decker. Both the Panther Cub and the Swift, with their rear engines, offered a lower entrance but also a number of teething problems, so that by the time the single-deck Atlanteans arrived, which were Mark II examples, Leyland were beginning to get to grips with some of the complexities. Bodybuilders too were not without their own difficulties; the Panther Cubs were originally to have been bodied by Marshall, but in the event only a dozen were dealt with, the balance receiving MCW bodies. The fact that Portsmouth turned to AEC chassis after so long perhaps says more about the problems being experienced with the competitive chassis. The Swifts also had Marshall bodies, not an organisation with a longevity of bus building, whereas the single-deck Atlanteans received bodies by Seddon, a distinctly unusual combination.

By the time these single-deck buses had all been delivered the one-man-operation of double-decks had been legalised and in August 1969 Portsmouth modified the first of its rear-engined double-deckers for such work, Atlantean No. 202 being experimentally placed on service 17-18. From September 1969 until October 1970 all of Nos. 201-30 were adapted for their new role and to enable them to be operated with a driver only, the destination display was modified so that all destination changes could be made from the cab.

The A - Z of Portsmouth's bus routes

Since the lettered routes disappeared at this point in our story, the next few pages have been devoted to a retrospect of some of these services. Whilst the use of letters (rather than numerals) to identify services was by no means unique to the city, their uni-directional use probably falls into this classification.

The use of the letter 'A' on this bus service appears to have dated from 1927. Operating on this service towards the end of its life is Craven-bodied Leyland TD4 No. 138. *(STA)*
The instantly recognisable (of 40 years ago!) Guildhall Square is the location of all-Leyland No. 76 on service A.

Operating on service B (the reverse of the A) is Portsmouth's first Reading-bodied bus, No. 199 ,on Southsea front and passing an almost new BUT trolleybus, with side blind in use, on service 4. *(STA)*

A fine rear view of Leyland PD2 No. 64 at the Stanley Avenue terminus of service D. After arriving at the Dockyard this service would continue to Ferry Road. The bus has recently been out-shopped with a white roof. Trolleybus powers were obtained for an extension from Copnor Bridge to this point and the detailed overhead plans for this section were produced before the proposals were shelved.

The blinds are set for service D in this maker's official view of the second of the Reading-bodied buses which is posed on Southsea Common. *(STA)*

Crossley No. 32 stands at Madeira Road on service G to Moneyfield Avenue. This was a relatively short-lived terminus off the main route at Tangier Road.

Two views of service H at the canoe lake terminus at South Parade Pier, and which perhaps illustrate the complexity of Portsmouth's displays! Above Crossley No. 42 incorrectly shows the panel for the all year service (Green Lane – Eastern Avenue/Road) depending on the ultimate screen fitted, whilst, below, Leyland PD2 No. 100, in as delivered condition, with large fleet number, correctly shows the summer extension panel for the return journey from South Parade Pier to Eastern Avenue/Road and thereon to Green Lane (the screen would be changed to that shown on 42 *en route*).

Two views at Cosham Railway Station of the J and the K which also allows a comparison of bodywork on the Leyland version (on No. 130 above) and English Electric one (on No. 116 below) on these 1935 Leyland TD4s. Space does not permit an explanation of the rather complicated history of these two services which strictly speaking were not a pair. *(RM both)*

Leyland TD4 No. 123 operates on service M, which became the 148 group of services in 1955. It is seen at the All Saints Church stop in Commercial Road. *(RM)*

Crossley No. 57, in as-delivered condition on service O to Tipner. Services O-P were, with the A-B, the last lettered services to operate for the Corporation. *(ABC)*

The O-P was, with the A-B, to be redesignated 14-13, 1-2 respectively when the trolleybuses disappeared in July 1963. Crossley No.47, EBK 580, on service P to Locksway Road at St Marys Church. *(ABC)*

In another view taken outside Southdown's Hilsea garage, Leyland TD4 with Craven body, No. 139 heads towards Southsea on route S. This section of the R-S was replaced by the extension of the trolleybus service 5-6 on 25th May 1952. Uniquely for a Corporation service, the southbound journey (on service R) did not divert at Cosham into the compound but followed Southdown routes by travelling along Northern Road direct. *(RM)*

A reasonable load of passengers wait to board No. 229, 229 CRV, at the Greetham Street stop at the Guildhall. Having started its journey at Alexandra Park, on arrival at Eastney this bus will continue on via Albert Road and Bradford Junction to the Guildhall (again) and then retrace its steps to Alexandra Park and then continue via Northern Parade to Cosham Railway Station. With routes like this, it is perhaps not surprising that for many years the department allocated a route number for each direction to assist its passengers.

In typical Portsmouth fleet condition for the time, No. 231, 231 CRV, loads in Commercial Road for the Dockyard, having travelled into the city from Leigh Park.

Portsmouth's final order for Metro-Cammell double-deckers arrived in 1966 when nine more Leyland Atlanteans were delivered. Here No. 251, ERV 251D, operates on service 1, which had been lettered A until the day the trolleybuses finally operated.

About to negotiate a level crossing in Edinburgh Road, where a line led into the HM Dockyard, is No. 246, ERV 246D, one of nine Atlanteans delivered in 1966. Five of this batch were later to be converted to open-top. *(STA)*

Although the push for greater economies was in full swing by 1967, the use of double-deckers for one-man-operation was not permitted, and so Portsmouth turned to high capacity single-deckers in that year. Twenty five Leyland Panther Cubs were taken into stock that year and the first examples, which totalled a dozen, had bodies by Marshall, typified by No. 153, GTP 153E

The balance of the Panther Cubs were bodied by Metro-Cammell and No. 165, GTP 165F, although entering service in 1967, carried an 'F' suffix registration mark as it entered service after 1st August that year, the 'E' suffix only being used for seven months.

A significant change occurred in 1969 when the very first batch of AEC motor buses entered the fleet after 50 years. They were AEC Swifts and were also bodied by Marshall. At the time, this combination of manufacturers was incidentally finding favour in the Capital, though not for long!

In due course the AEC Swifts also wore a revised livery as shown by No. 180, NTP 180H. The influence of the designer-styled lettering on the blinds suggests once again that those who dream up these schemes are not users of the buses.

One-man-operation, using Leyland Atlanteans, resulted in the vehicles having to be modified for this purpose and No. 217, 217 BTP, which was rebuilt in 1970, had its destination display reduced as a result. It is seen negotiating the roundabout at Spur Road, Cosham. *(ABC)*

From the end of 1971 the Atlanteans began appearing in a revised livery with greater areas of white applied to the livery and an elimination of the lining out. A new City crest also adorns the side of the bus. Number 213, 213 BTP, passes through Hilsea in its new corporate colours.

7 – The Seventies

The first complete service to be converted to double-deck one-man-operation was the 145 which, apart from the elimination of a conductor from 23rd March 1970, was also cut back from Old Portsmouth to the Guildhall. The Old Portsmouth section was covered by the diversion of the 12B which had been terminating at the Dockyard. It was now redesignated 21 and the section from Copnor Bridge followed exactly the same route as the original 15-16 trolleybus service. The same date saw the 19-20 restricted to operate Guildhall to Cosham Railway Station during the off-peak. A major change to evening services was introduced on 22nd November 1970, which included further extensions to driver only operation. It would seem that these changes were driven by the need for economies, as most operators would tend to refrain from making changes a month before Christmas during what would normally be the busiest time in the year for passenger traffic. During this period the Department continually strived to produce a network which matched the customer requirements at minimal cost. The result was continual changes to the services, it must be said on occasions to the bewilderment of the public. For probably the first time on a wholesale basis the historic duplication of route numbers, depending on the direction of travel, was abandoned. Thus 5-6, 7-8, 11-12, 13-14 and 15-16 became the 6, 7, 11, 14 and 16 respectively, the latter being considerably extended, evenings and Sundays although a new service 8, operating from Clarence Pier via Fratton and Stubbington Avenue to Devon Road, was introduced. The 9-10 disappeared completely and the 23-24 was merged with the 22 to become 22-23. At the same time the 19-20 was extended from Cosham to Wymering as 20 or 20A, depending on the route in Wymering. Southbound services were numbered 19.

A 'modification' of a different sort involved Atlantean 249 which appeared in August 1971 as an over-all advertising bus – the first in the fleet – for the Tricorn Centre. Different is perhaps an understatement and its unpopularity was probably only matched by the shopping centre it was promoting. Fortunately, both grotesque apparitions are no longer with us; the bus was soon repainted and was the first in the 'greater white'

livery in December that year. The concrete edifice lasted until the 21st Century before being finally demolished, in 2004.

By 1971 the 36-year old Leylands on the seafront Service were clearly showing their age, despite having acquired a new livery of ivory with three maroon bands in 1968, and the department selected some of the 1956 PD2s as their replacements. With the conversion of PD2 No. 96 and its renumbering to 6 in 1972, the last TD4 was withdrawn. Happily all four entered into preservation. The route for which they had been converted had also seen changes, the service being extended from Clarence Pier to Old Portsmouth for the 1967 season and to the Dockyard for the 1971 season. It operated as two overlapping services from this time; from Hayling Ferry to the Dockyard and from South Parade Pier to Old Portsmouth. The other seasonal seafront service, the 26, which ran to Hayling Ferry from Eastney finally succumbed after 30th August 1971, although staff shortages had made its operation sporadic at the end to say the least.

From the earliest days of the trams the destination 'DOCKYARD' had been in use, although we have seen that during the war it was not favoured by the authorities. Changes in Naval administration in the 1970s resulted in the Dockyard (the civilian manned ship re-fitting facility) becoming part of HM Naval Base headed by a Port Admiral. 'DOCKYARD' was deemed an inappropriate destination given the new Naval Base structure and therefore the longstanding destination on buses was changed to become 'The Hard', the actual thoroughfare on which the buses terminated.

The next new vehicles to arrive reverted to double-deckers of the improved AN68 Atlantean variety. They were the first double-deckers suitable for use as one-person-operation from new and were fitted with dual doors like the single-deckers, and introduced yet another new body manufacturer to the fleet, having been built in Scotland by Alexander at Falkirk. A total of 90 (Nos. 255-344) of this combination entered service between September 1972 and November 1979 permitting the conversion of all services, bar the seafront Service, to driver only operation. The 3-4 had been so converted, with double-deckers, on 23rd January 1972 and the 148 followed on 15th October that year. It was the turn of service 143 to receive this treatment from 30th August

Standing at the Portchester terminus of the 145 at Cornaway Lane, this 1956 Leyland No. 94, LRV 986, has received the more attractive white roof by the time this picture was taken. *(ABC)*

In 1968 the then four-open-top buses in the fleet were given a revised livery of ivory with three maroon bands. Number 6 is seen at the Hayling Ferry terminus, after the service had been extended from Clarence Pier to Point, Old Portsmouth, as the Floating Bridge terminus was now known.

'Before and after' picture of two of the 1956 Leylands. On the left, No. 1, LRV 991, and formerly No. 99 without a roof and on the right, No. 94, LRV 986, in final version of the livery, with roof.

The final single-deckers to arrive, in 1971, before orders reverted to Leyland Atlanteans (of the AN68 variety) were undoubtedly unusual buses by any standards as they were a dozen Leyland Atlantean PDR2/1 models with single-deck bodies built by Seddon of Oldham. With a backdrop that should no longer be unfamiliar to the reader, No. 189, RTP 189J, is operating on what was Portsmouth's last trolleybus route, closed a mere seven years previously.

An off-side view of a single-deck Atlantean and travelling along Park Road by the side of the Southern Region railway line from Portsmouth Harbour is No. 196, TBK 196K. The destination display is slightly unusual in that no route number is shown. *(STA)*

The first Leyland Atlantean AN68 buses were delivered in 1972 and with bodywork by Alexander of Falkirk introduced yet another manufacturer to the fleet. This combination was eventually to total some 90 units for the operator, and No. 270, VTP 270L, was one of 18 vehicles from the first order.

1973. The last 25 of these AN68s were fitted with automatic transmission and power steering.

Mr Botterill moved to Edinburgh in 1973 and was followed as General Manager by his deputy, Mr D Racher. To complete this aspect of the management story up to the end of direct municipal ownership days, it should be recorded that Mr E Boyes, who had been Deputy Manager at Blackburn, took over in 1979.

Further modification of Atlanteans to make them suitable for one-man-operation took place between April and August 1974 when Nos. 251-4 were converted. However, in 1975 withdrawal of the first of the rear-engined double-deckers occurred and interestingly for the time a small number were sold to another municipal undertaking, East Staffordshire, which until local government reorganisation the previous year had been better known as Burton Corporation. During 1975 to 1976 and again in 1978 and 1979, in an echo of wartime events, a number of these Atlanteans were also hired to Hants & Dorset Motor Services.

During 1976 the single-deck fleet had undergone an interesting change. That year the last of the high floor Leylands were withdrawn and in their place 14 dual-door Leyland Nationals entered the fleet. If the early Atlanteans from Leyland had caused the engineers difficulties, not only in Portsmouth, then nationally, the Nationals would appear to have been no easier. In fact their departure after only five years from Portsmouth would seem to support this view regarding their popularity.

On a more positive note, 17th June 1976 saw the opening of the Continental Ferry Port, a very real indication of the changing face of Portsmouth. The first vehicle to come off the Brittany Ferries' inaugural voyage was no less a bus than open-top Leyland PD2 No. 6. The new port was to require special facilities which saw trailers used on buses operating between there and Portsmouth Harbour Station. The associated provision of new highways serving the new port included the opening of the M275 and before long express bus services into Portsmouth were making use of this facility. The days of Portsbridge being the only entry to the city were well and truly superseded.

Virtually throughout the whole of 1977 work continued to modify the Leyland Atlantean fleet to make them suitable for driver only operation and Nos. 236-48 were dealt with during this period. The introduction of the summer timetable on 1st

May that year, itself postponed for a month for operational reasons that are now not clear, saw another fairly extensive revision of services which included the withdrawal of the 6 and the 16. In the case of the former alternate journeys on 1-2 were diverted via Eastney as 1A-2A to compensate for its loss and this service was converted to double-deck one-man-operation. The 7-8 and 19-20 were linked and renumbered 9-10, with some journeys on service 3 being diverted in Paulsgrove to cover the erstwhile 19-20. The 22-23 Cosham local services were replaced by a group of services numbered 5, 6, 7 and 8. Perhaps surprisingly, the 145 from Portchester was renumbered 21, a move away from numbers in the Southdown series with its other terminus now at Winston Churchill Avenue. This 21 should not be confused with the former 12B service 21 of March 1970. By this time the 13-14 ran to Point Old Portsmouth via a different route. It was also diverted via Cosham Railway Station. The 11 and 12 were also rerouted and rather interestingly converted back to crew operation and this became the last regular service to require conductors until they ceased to be used from July 1979.

For the summer season from 5th June 1977 (the same day as the seasonal 25 service commenced that year) a new City Tour was introduced in conjunction with the City Museums Department. They provided guides who gave a commentary and the tour commenced from South Parade Pier. Besides passing through the Dockyard (no stop was made) it also travelled along part of Portsdown Hill at Fort Widley, which gave unrivalled views over the City and the Solent. The Silver Jubilee of the accession of Queen Elizabeth II was widely celebrated in 1977, and again a Naval Fleet Review was held in the Solent, although nowhere near on the scale of the 1953 event. This time a vehicle festooned with lights was not to tour the City (as had been the case 24 years before), but the six Leyland PD2 open-top buses were given a modified commemorative livery in May that year, the same month that the first of the next generation of open-top buses for the seafront service emerged. It was No. 254 which became No. 7 in the open-top series. Ultimately, four more of this final batch of Leyland PDR1/1s were to be similarly converted.

As previously indicated, it has not been possible to record every service change during this period of the department's history as so many alterations were being made and as an example, from 30th January 1978 there was more fine tuning of the Cosham local routes numbered 5 to 8, which had only been introduced the previous summer. A major revision of the services to Leigh Park was introduced from 18th March 1979 which saw the introduction of new service 24 from The Hard to Havant. As early as 1944 various schemes were developed for improved loading arrangements at the Dockyard including plans for a Bus Station but to no avail. In 1969 further proposals for a modern facility at the Dockyard terminus (already now termed 'The Hard', of course) to improve interchange between buses, trains and ferries were made. After a long gestation period, it was officially opened on 18th May 1979. It was built over the open water in the triangle between the railway line, the elevated approach road to Portsmouth Harbour Station and The Hard.

All services which formerly terminated at The Hard outside the Dockyard were transferred to the new Interchange. Open-top No. 10 is seen using its new stand at this location. In the background the chimneys of Portsmouth power station (now demolished) may be seen; this was a feature of Portsmouth's skyline for many years. The railway carriage in the background confirms the close proximity of Portsmouth Harbour Station.

Portsmouth Football Matches

Don't miss the kick-off! Special buses are operated to all league matches at the **Fratton Park Ground** — From various points in the Portsmouth area

For full details of fares and departure times please enquire at local Southdown or Portsmouth Corporation offices

57

PORTSMOUTH JOINT TRANSPORT SERVICES
(CITY AREA)

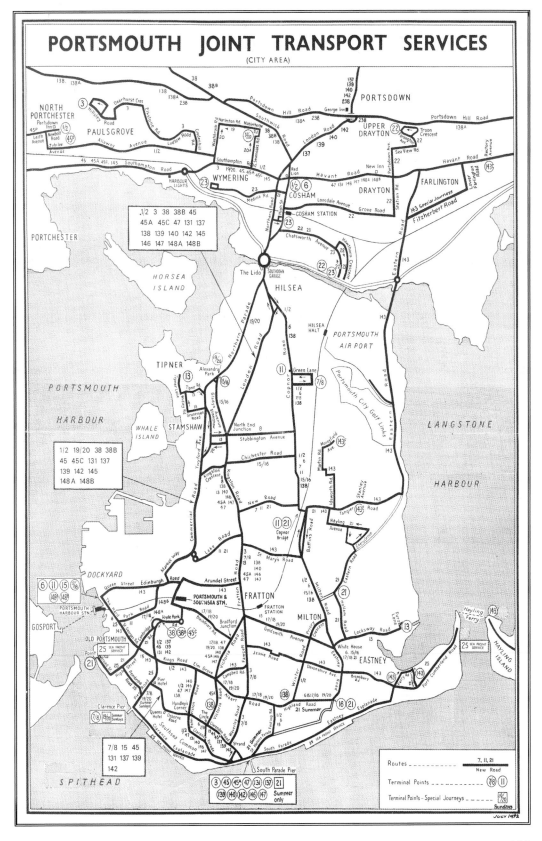

The all-conquering Leyland National arrived in Portsmouth's fleet in 1976, when 14 Mark 1 examples were taken into stock. Number 104, KCR 104, is seen at the Dockyard. As explained in the text, the duration of these vehicles in the fleet was relatively short.

Wearing Silver Jubilee livery No. 5, (ex 94) LRV 986, displays both 'The Hard' and 'Dockyard' on its destination blinds as it passes South Parade Pier.

The penultimate batch of Alexander-bodied Atlanteans arrived in early 1979 and totalled 15 buses, the second of which No. 321, UOR 321T, is depicted.

The final ten buses of this combination were delivered at the end of 1979 and the last one of all, No. 344, YBK 344V, is pictured at Queen Alexandra Hospital on service 2.

Delivered in1966 was No. 252, ERV 252D, seen here approaching Milton White House. In 1979 this bus was converted to open-top, with considerable more protection for the upper-deck passengers than had ever been thought necessary when the Leyland TD4s were so treated, and renumbered 10.

For many years one of the most popular events in the bus rally season was the Southsea Spectacular, held every year on Southsea Common. Open-top Atlantean No. 10 is seen here attending the rally, which was well supported by the Transport Department during the period the event was held, as well as by vehicles attending from considerable distances in many cases, in the days when fuel costs were not such a consideration.

8 – The Eighties

As has already been seen, during the 1970s there had been many changes to the bus services, largely due to the significant decline in passengers resulting in a reduction in miles operated over the previous decade. The 1980s, however, saw the greatest changes to the Transport Department. With the conversion of the seafront Service to one-person-operation the elimination of conductors was completed. The need for economies was still overwhelming when one looked at just two significant statistics. In 20 years number of passengers carried had halved to 30m and mileage fell by 2,500,000. The 1980 deliveries saw three more Leyland Nationals taken into stock, but this time they were of the improved Mark 2 variety and had only one door and dual-purpose seating with a view to their use on private hire work which the department was trying to develop. The final Leyland Atlanteans also arrived; ten in number with yet another new bodybuilder to the fleet. East Lancashire provided the two-door bodies to their standard but attractive style.

Eric Boyes' arrival in 1979 has already been recorded but one of the major tasks he had to deal with initially concerned the financial health of the undertaking. The National Bus Company, in dealing with similar problems in its own subsidiaries, had developed what it termed a Market Analysis Project (MAP) which was an attempt to match the services it provided with the passengers who were looking to travel. In due course Southdown took up this programme and since the Corporation agreement was virtually a 50/50 one in Portsmouth it was inevitable that they should become involved. From the Corporation's point of view, the financial objectives of an NBC subsidiary were not necessarily those of a municipal trading department and it could be that the seeds of the Corporation Transport's future and ultimate demise were sown at this time. When the MAP exercise was complete the results were to be the withdrawal of all the single-deckers delivered between1969 and 1976, with the exception of a handful of the Seddon-bodied Atlanteans (in fact, there was a reduction in requirement of no less than 38 buses), redundancies, major changes in services, far too extensive to be listed here and the closure of North End depot on 31st October 1981 after over 100 years of use. Although the remaining fleet could

all be accommodated at Eastney, Leigh Park was retained to reduce empty mileage. Over the next five years only seven more buses were taken into stock. As far as the city generally was concerned changes nationally, both economic and political, including the end of the 'Cold War', saw an alteration to the requirements for industry and a reduction in defence spending, both of which hit Portsmouth quite severely. By the 1980s Southsea, along with many other resorts, was suffering from the loss of the traditional holiday maker market, and to cater for more sophisticated tastes increasing emphasis was placed on the City's maritime and military history. The Tudor Warship the Mary Rose, which had been raised from the seabed just off Southsea in 1982, was put on display the following year, and much was made of the 40th Anniversary of D-Day in June 1984 and the local involvement in this event. After eight years restoration HMS Warrior was to be opened as another exhibit next to the Dockyard in 1987 and the Royal Marine Museum was developed at Eastney. Whilst all this was commendable, they were not really developments which were going to aid the Transport Department to any degree. The undertaking thus approached Deregulation in 1986 in less than an ideal state.

The fleet was reasonably modern but since the effects of MAP had eliminated the post-1976 single-deck vehicles. The double-deck fleet included some 60 examples of 1972-75 vintage, all of which ideally needed replacing by 1986. For the record, four more Mark 2 Nationals had entered the fleet in 1981 and three Dennis Lancets arrived the year after. Finally, in 1986 a second-hand coach was acquired via a dealer. The joint agreement with Southdown, which although a bit like the curate's egg, had on balance served the department quite well. Deregulation was to end the formal agreement with Southdown. Like every other local authority-owned bus undertaking in Great Britain, the City Council was obliged to set up an arms length company to take over the Council undertaking from 26th October 1986, so in this case Portsmouth City Transport Limited was formed. There was some investigation to explore the possibility of setting up a company to include both the City Transport and Southdown operation in Portsmouth, but the government of the day were not in favour of this. Whatever else was to happen, the story of the City of Portsmouth Passenger Transport Department was at an end.

115

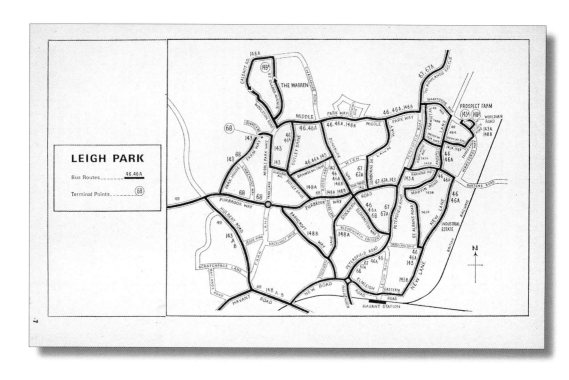

LEIGH PARK

Bus Routes _____ **46.46A**

Terminal Points _____ (68)

Reference has been made in the text to the rather complicated route arrangements in Leigh Park involving the 148 group of services, and this 1972 diagram, above, underlines the service complexity. Reference has also been made to the extensive changes brought about by the introduction of the National Bus Company's MAP alterations in November 1981, and the extracts from this contemporary leaflet shown opposite perhaps give some indication of the scale of the revisions.

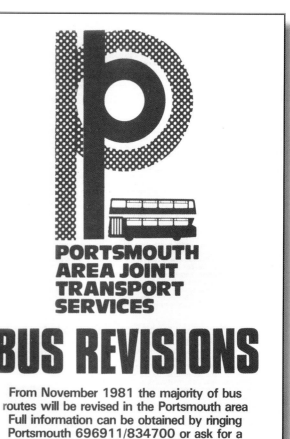

PORTSMOUTH AREA JOINT TRANSPORT SERVICES

BUS REVISIONS

From November 1981 the majority of bus routes will be revised in the Portsmouth area Full information can be obtained by ringing Portsmouth 696911/834700 or ask for a new bus guide

WHY CHANGE SERVICES ANYWAY?

You may recall the Market Analysis Project (MAP) which we undertook in the Portsmouth area. This survey together with comments we have received following consultation meetings has given us the opportunity to tailor the **Portsmouth Area Joint Transport Services** to meet, where economically possible, the Public need; within the financial constraints placed upon us. This leaflet briefly describes the service changes, area by area.

NORTH OF WATERLOOVILLE

HAMBLEDON and **DENMEAD** will continue to be served by Service 745 operating hourly each day via the existing route to Waterlooville and then via Elizabeth Road and Park Avenue to Cosham and Portsmouth.
PETERSFIELD, CLANFIELD and **HORNDEAN** will be served by Services 741, 743. Service 741 will be revised to operate between Clanfield and Southsea via Horndean and Hazleton Way each hour. Service 743 will continue to operate between Petersfield and Southsea via Horndean and London Road each hour, except on Sundays when the service will terminate at Clanfield. These services combine to give a half hourly service from Clanfield (Hourly evenings and Sundays).
CLANFIELD will also be served by new Service 742 operating via **CATHERINGTON** every two hours off peak, to Waterlooville, Portsmouth and Southsea.
LOVEDEAN, WECOCK FARM, will be served by existing Services 308,309 and by Services 740, 742, 744 and 746. New Service 746 will operate from Lovedean, Day Lane every two hours, except evenings and Sundays, combining with Services 308, 309 and 742 at the junction of Lovedean Lane/Milton Road to give a half hourly service along the length of Milton Road to Waterlooville. Services 742 and 746 continue via Park Avenue to Cosham and Portsmouth. Eagle Avenue, Hart Plain Avenue will be served by Services 740, 744 increasing the service to every 15 minutes to Waterlooville (half hourly evenings/Sundays). Service 740 proceeds via London Road to Cosham and Portsmouth. Service 744 via Crookhorn, with alternate off peak journeys serving Upper Drayton and Havant Road.

WATERLOOVILLE/STAKES/PURBROOK/ CROOKHORN

The combined services from **WATERLOOVILLE** to **PORTSMOUTH** and **SOUTHSEA** are Services 740-746. Services 740, 741 and 743 give a 15 minute service down London Road through **PURBROOK** (Half hourly evenings/Sundays) and are revised to observe all stops north of Cosham.
Services 742, 745, 746 combine to give a half hourly service along Elizabeth Road and Park Avenue replacing Services 337 and 338 (Hourly evenings/Sundays).
Service 744 operates via **STAKES** and **CROOKHORN** (Hourly evenings/Sundays).
All Services 740-746 follow a new route south of Cosham via London Road, Kingston Road, Lake Road, Commercial Road, Winston Churchill Avenue, Kings Road, Palmerston Road, The Strand to Southsea, South Parade Pier.

DROXFORD/WICKHAM/SOUTHWICK

These communities will continue to be provided for by Service 350 along the existing route with a revised peak and off peak timetable. *H.M.S. DRYAD* will be served by a peak only Service 450.

FAREHAM/PORTCHESTER

FAREHAM will continue to be served by Services X16 and Service 347, each operating every half hour (Hourly evenings/Sundays), between Fareham and Southsea. Service X16 will operate via Cosham and Hilsea, and together with 347 will replace Services 213, 214 between PORTCHESTER and PORTSMOUTH. This will give four buses per hour between Fareham, Portchester and Cosham (two per hour evenings/Sundays).
Service X16 will continue to operate hourly West of Fareham to Southampton except on Sundays.
An experimental Service 353 will operate between Fareham, Portchester, Paulsgrove, Cosham and Havant to provide a new off-peak shopping link.

ROWLANDS CASTLE

Service 327 will continue to operate between Havant and Rowlands Castle with certain peak journeys extended to Horndean. Frequency will remain hourly.

WESTBOURNE/SOUTHBOURNE/EMSWORTH

New Services 328, 329 and existing Service 700 will replace existing Services 331, 332 and 357. Service 328 will operate a clockwise loop over the existing 332/357 route through **DENVILLES** to **WESTBOURNE,** Cricketers then continuing through to **SOUTHBOURNE** returning via **EMSWORTH** to Havant. Service 329 will operate over the same route in an anti-clockwise direction. Both 328, 329 will operate hourly and together with Service 700 provide a half hourly service between Havant and Emsworth.

HAYLING ISLAND

Will continue to be served by Services 300, 301, 302, 310, 311 and 702, each operating via existing routes and frequencies with minor timetable adjustments.

LEIGH PARK/HAVANT

WARREN PARK will be served by Service 23 operating every half hour to **HAVANT, COSHAM** and **SOUTHSEA,** with alternate journeys serving Woolston or Swanmore Road, replacing Services 313, 323.
Revised Services 313, 323 will route a circular route to and from Havant via Bedhampton Way, Purbrook Way, Park House Farm Way, Botley Drive, and Dunsbury Way, hourly in each direction except evenings and Sundays.

Services through Goldsmith Avenue will operate as Service 13A-14A between Furze Lane and Commercial Road, and Services 17-18 between Eastney and Commercial Road. The 13-14 link to Portchester as Service 213-214 will be withdrawn. Service 347 will operate from Bradford Junction to Portchester and Fareham via Fratton and Cosham.
Services operating via Milton Road past St Mary's Hospital will be provided by Services 1-2 or 3-4 and 15.

BUCKLAND/KINGSTON/FRATTON

Services 1-2, 22, 700 and X16 will continue to operate via Kingston Crescent and Mile End Road to Commercial Road and The Hard or Southsea, with Services 7-8/8A and 51 providing part buses along Mile End Road.
Services 23, 740 to 746 will operate via Kingston Road and Lake Road to Commercial Road and The Hard or Southsea with additional buses being provided by Service 13-14 through Lake Road to Old Portsmouth.
'Fratton Road' buses will be provided by Service 3-4 via Arundel Street with Services 11-12 and 16-16A/16B. Services 3-4, 7-8 and 347 will operate to Southsea via Elm Grove and Palmerston Road (3-4 and 347) or Fawcett Road and The Strand (7-8). In the evenings and Sundays Service 3-4 will operate via Fawcett Road to South Parade Pier replacing Service 7-8 which will not operate at these times.

SOUTHSEA

Regular services will operate to Commercial Road, Fratton Road, The Hard and most parts of the City and beyond to Havant, Leigh Park, Waterlooville and Fareham.
Services 1-2, 3-4, 23 and 51 will operate via Clarence Parade and Palmerston Road; Services 7-8, 15, 52, 740 and 746 will operate via Clarendon Road. Buses in the Kings Road and Elm Grove areas will be provided by services 3-4, 347 to Fratton; 23 and 740 to 746 to Commercial Road; Service 16-16A/16B to The Hard and Commercial Road or Eastney.
Services 1-2 and 7-8 will operate via Western Parade and The Terraces to Commercial Road; and Service 15 operating via Duisburg Way to Old Portsmouth and The Hard.

OLD PORTSMOUTH

Service 13-14 will continue to operate from The Point to Commercial Road and Copnor every 30 minutes and hourly in the evenings and on Sundays. Service 15 will operate daily every 30 minutes to The Hard or Palmerston Road, Southsea and Eastney. Service 16-16A/16B will operate every 30 minutes to The Hard, Commercial Road, Milton and beyond, or Elm Grove and Eastney.

THE HARD/PORTSEA/COMMERCIAL ROAD

Regular services will operate between The Hard and Commercial Road to all parts of the City and beyond. Improved links will operate to Havant via Cosham and Farlington, and additional buses will operate on new Service 13A-14A to Milton and Locksway Road.

There are no route alterations to the following services although some timings will be revised, 1-2, 11-12, 15, 17-18, 51, 300, 301, 302, 310, 311, 308, 309, 347, 350, 361, 362, 450, 452, 453, 702.
From Sunday November 1st, the following services will be revised and new services introduced, 7, 8, 22, 23, 24, 52, 313, 314, 323, 324, 327, 328, 329, 353, X16, 740, 741, 742, 743, 744, 745, 746.
The following service numbers will be discontinued:
5, 6, 9, 10, 213, 214, 330, 331, 332, 335, 336, 337, 338, 357, 367, 731, 733, 735.

Further information telephone:
Portsmouth 834700 Eastney Depot and City Transport Offices
Portsmouth 696911 Southdown Offices
Portsmouth 755266 The Hard Interchange.

In 1980 the Corporation turned to East Lancs to body what turned out to be its last Leyland Atlanteans. There were ten units in the order and the last of them, No. 354, CPO 354W ,is seen here. *(STA)*

Just as the first delivery of Mark I Leyland Nationals were about to be withdrawn a further trio, but this time of the Mark 2 variety, entered service in 1981. As was the custom at the time, they were delivered in all-over white and the, by now, minimum amount of scarlet was added by the operator. Compared with the previous ones, these Nationals had a single door and seats for 41; No. 116, ERV 116V, is caught post-deregulation at Hilsea.

Portsmouth's story had almost turned full circle when, in 1982, the department returned to Wadham for motorbus bodies. Admittedly the factory had moved and this order was for only three single-deckers, but again there was a connection with the early days in that the chassis on this trio were supplied by Dennis of Guildford. In the upper view is No.95, GTP 95X, the only one of the trio to have dual-purpose seating, while below the last one, No. 97, GTP 97X, is in Eastney depot. They had seats for 33 and 35 respectively.

Fleet List

TRAMS						
YEAR	FLEET Nos.	TYPE	TRUCKS	BODY	SEATS	NOTES
1901	1 -44	Open-top 4-wheel	Brill 21E	ERTCW	55	
1902	45-80	Open-top 4-wheel	Brill 21E	ERTCW	55	
1904	81-84	Open-top 4-wheel	Brill 21E	PCT/Milnes	46	a
1907	85-100	Open-top 4-wheel	Brill 21E	Dick Kerr	54	
1919	104	Single-deck 4-wheel	Brill 21E	SCT/Dick Kerr	40	b
1920	105-16	Fully-enclosed 4-wheel	EEC	English Electric	58	
1931	1	Fully-enclosed 4-wheel	Peckham	PCT	58	c

Notes
a - rebuilt from former horse tramcars
b - originally Southampton Corporation 48-seat open-top; rebuilt to toastrack 1913
c - sold to Sunderland Corporation

TROLLEYBUSES						
YEAR	REG Nos.	FLEET Nos.	CHASSIS	ELEC EQUIP	BODY	NOTES
1934	RV 4649-52	1-4	AEC 661T	EEC	English Electric H50R	
1934	RV 4653-5	5-7	Leyland TBD2	GEC	English Electric H50R	
1934	RV 4656	8	Sunbeam MF2	BTH	English Electric H50R	
1934	RV 4657	9	Karrier E4	EEC	English Electric H50R	
1934	RV 4660	10	Sunbeam MF2	BTH	Metro-Cammell H50R	
1934	RV 4661	11	Karrier E4	BTH	Metro-Cammell H50R	
1934	RV 4658	12	AEC 663T	EEC	English Electric H60R	
1934	RV 4659	13	Sunbeam MS3	BTH	English Electric H60R	
1934	RV 4662	14	Sunbeam MS3	BTH	Metro-Cammell H60R	
1934	RV 4663	15	AEC 663T	EEC	Metro-Cammell H60R	
1935	RV 6374-82	16-25	AEC 661T	EEC	English Electric H50R	
1936	RV 8307-36	25-54	AEC 661T	EEC	Craven H52R	
1936	RV 9106-41	55-90	AEC 661T	EEC	Craven H52R	
1937	RV 9142-5/9-54	91-100	AEC 661T	EEC	Craven H52R	
1950/1	ERV 926-40	301-15	BUT 9611T	EEC	Burlingham H52R	

Nos. 1-100 renumbered 201-300 in 1938

SOUTH PARADE PIER. SOUTHSEA.   D/11831

One can only have a high regard for the enthusiasm and patience of those who have restored and preserved historic motorbuses over the years, but how much more admiration must there be for those who have chosen to collect trams and trolleybuses. Two of the latter from Portsmouth's fleet have survived and above, the very first trolleybus, an AEC with English Electric bodywork, No. 201, carrying its post-1938 number, is seen at the Montague Motor Museum at Beaulieu, where it could be viewed in the 1960's. The only post-war trolleybus to survive is BUT No. 313, below. Originally sold for scrap in 1963 to a dealer in Hilsea, it was subsequently saved for preservation in 1965 and in April 1967 was operated on a tour of Bournemouth, where it is seen once more by the sea.

Captured on camera in 1925, long before any thoughts of conversion to a non-psv use were ever considered, let alone preservation as a passenger carrying vehicle, Thornycroft No. 10 is seen with its Wadham body operating on the original motorbus service to Devonshire Road. *(STA)*

The previous picture of a Karrier WL6 (see page 17) was also taken at Cosham, as is this view. From the angle photographed it is not been possible to identify which of the Brush-bodied examples is portrayed in this picture. *(STA)*

MOTOR BUSES					
YEAR	REG Nos.	FLEET Nos.	CHASSIS	BODY	NOTES
1919	BK 2978/7/9-86	1-10	Thornycroft J	Wadham O34R	a
1924	TP 115-9	11-5	Guy J	Wadham T15	
1924	TP 181-3	16-8	Dennis 50-cwt	Strachan & Brown B20F	
1924	TP 186-9	19-22	Dennis 50-cwt	Strachan & Brown B25F	
1925	TP 751-61/5	23-34	Dennis 50-cwt	Dennis B26F	
1926	LF 9344	35	AEC B	Dodson O34R	b
1927	TP 4422/3	36/7	Dennis E	Ransomes, Sims & Jefferies B32F	
1927	TP 4812/-3	38/9	Karrier CL6	Ransomes, Sims & Jefferies B39F	
1927	TP 4703-5	40-2	Karrier WL6/2	Brush H60R	
1927	TP 4832-6	43-7	Karrier WL6/2	Brush H60R	
1928	TP 6872-7	48-53	Karrier WL6/2	English Electric H60R	
1928	TP 6864-71	54-61	Dennis E	Davidson B32R	
1929	TP 8098-101	62-5	Dennis EV	Hall Lewis B32R	
1929	TP 8102/3	66/7	Dennis EV	Portsmouth Comm Motors B32R	
1929	TP 8091-4	68-71	Thornycroft BC	Hall Lewis B32R	
1929	TP 8095/7	72/3	Thornycroft BC	Wadham B32R	
1931	RV 236/7	1/2	Tilling-Stevens	Park Royal B30R	
1931	RV 238	3	Leyland LT2	Park Royal B30R	
1931	RV 241-3	4-6	Leyland TD1	Short H50R	
1931	RV 715/6	7/8	Leyland TD1	Park Royal H50R	
1931	RV 717/8	9/10	Leyland TD1	Short H50R	
1931	RV 719	35	AEC Regent	Short H50R	
1931	RV 720	74	Crossley Condor	Short H50R	
1932	RV 1135-7/41-7	75-84	TSM E6OA6	English Electric H50R	
1932	RV 1138-40/29/8/30-4	85-94	Leyland TD1	English Electric H50R	
1932	RV 1990-2009	95-114	Crossley Condor	English Electric H50R	
1933	RV 3410-21	16-27	Leyland TD2	English Electric H50R	
1935	JG 522	52	Daimler Limousine	Daimler 6	c
1935	RV 6358-68	115-25	Leyland TD4	English Electric H50R	d
1935	RV 6369	126	Leyland TD4c	English Electric H50R	
1935	RV 6370-2	127-9	Leyland TD4	Leyland H50R	e
1935	RV 6373	130	Leyland TD4c	Leyland H50R	
1936/7	RV 9385-9414	131-60	Leyland TD4	Cravens H50R	
1939	BTP 941-6	41-6	Leyland LZ4	Wadham B32R	
1942	CTP 3	161	Bedford OWB	Duple B32F	
1943	CTP 19/41	162/3	Bedford OWB	Mulliner B32F	
1943/4	CTP 85-9/199/200	164-70	Bedford OWB	Duple B32F	
1944	CTP 151/2/67/75-80	171-9	Daimler CWA6	Duple H56R	f
1947	DTP 808/9	199/200	Leyland PD1A	Reading H52R	
1948	DTP 810	1	Leyland PD1	Reading H52R	
1948	DTP 811-3	2-4	Leyland PD1A	Reading H52R	
1948	EBK 23-6	11-4	Crossley DD42/5T	Reading H52R	
1948	DTP 814	180	Leyland PD1	Weymann H56R	
1948	DTP 815/6	181/2	Leyland PD1A	Weymann H56R	
1948	DTP 817-21	183-7	Leyland PD1	Weymann H56R	

123

Not all buses, following their retirement from active passenger service, necessarily went straight to the breaker's yard. In the upper picture, former bus No. 17 was converted, in 1952, to Tower Wagon TW1. After the closure of the trolleybus system it was retained as a breakdown tender until it was sold into preservation in 1975. Crossley Condor No. 105 became a departmental lorry in 1953 and was eventually scrapped in 1961.

YEAR	REG Nos.	FLEET Nos.	CHASSIS	BODY	NOTES
1948	DTP 822	188	Leyland PD1A	Weymann H56R	
1948	DTP 823	189	Leyland PD1	Weymann H56R	
1948	DTP 824-6	190-2	Leyland PD1A	Weymann H56R	
1948	DRV 107-10	193-6	Leyland PD1	Weymann H56R	
1948	DRV 111/2	197/8	Leyland PD1A	Weymann H56R	
1949	EBK 27/8	15/28	Crossley DD42/5T	Reading H52R	
1949	EBK 566-90	29-42/7-57	Crossley DD42/5T	Crossley H52R	g
1952	GTP 975-99	58-82	Leyland PD2/10	Leyland H56R	
1956	LRV 975-99	83-107	Leyland PD2/12	Metro-Cammell H56R	h
1958	ORV 985-99	108-22	Leyland PD2/40	Metro-Cammell H56R	
1959	STP 995-9	123-7	Leyland PD3/6	Metro-Cammell H64R	
1960	TTP 990-9	16-25	Leyland PSUC1/1	Weymann B34D	
1961	YBK 131-42	131-42	Leyland L1	Weymann B34D	
1963	143-9 BTP	143-9	Leyland L1	Weymann B41D	
1963	201-25 BTP	201-25	Leyland PDR1/1	Metro-Cammell H76F	
1963	226 -35 CRV	226-35	Leyland PDR1/1	Metro-Cammell H76F	
1964	BBK 236-45B	236-45	Leyland PDR1/1	Metro-Cammell H76F	
1966	ERV 246-54D	246-54	Leyland PDR1/1	Metro-Cammell H76F	i
1967	GTP 150-61E	150-61	Leyland PSURC1.1	Marshall B42D	
1967	GTP 162/3/72E	162/3/72	Leyland PSURC1.1	Metro-Cammell B42D	
1967	GTP 164-71/3-5F	164-71/3-5	Leyland PSURC1.1	Metro-Cammell B42D	
1969	NTP 176-87H	176-87	AEC Swift	Marshall B42D	
1971	RTP 188/9J	188/9	Leyland PDR2/1	Seddon B40D	
1971	TBK 190-9K	190-9	Leyland PDR2/1	Seddon B40D	
1972	VTP 255-72L	255-72	Leyland AN68/1R	Alexander H75D	
1973	XTP 273-93L	273-93	Leyland AN68/1R	Alexander H75D	
1975	GOT 294-301N	294-301	Leyland AN68/1R	Alexander H75D	
1975	HOR 302-19N	302-19	Leyland AN68/1R	Alexander H75D	
1976	KCR 101-14P	101-14	Leyland National	Leyland B38D	
1979	UOR 320-34T	320-34	Leyland AN68A/1R	Alexander H75D	
1979	YBK 335-44V	335-44	Leyland AN68A/1R	Alexander H75D	
1980	CPO 98-100W	98-100	Leyland National 2	Leyland DP40F	
1980	CPO 345-54W	345-54	Leyland AN68A/1R	East Lancs H73D	
1981	ERV 115-8W	115-8	Leyland National 2	Leyland DP40F	
1982	GTP 95X	95	Dennis Lancet	Wadham Stringer DP33F	
1982	GTP 96/7X	96/7	Dennis Lancet	Wadham Stringer B35F	
1986	AUS 644S	101	Leyland PSU5B/4R	Duple C57F	j

Notes
a - Nos. 1-10 rebodied with Dodson bodies ex LGOC ⅰBⅰ type in 1926
b - ex London General (No. B2017); re-registered BK 2342 in 1927
c - ex A Simmons, new 1929. Used on Airport service
d - Nos. 115, 117, 124/5 rebuilt to O50R in 1953-5 and renumbered 5-8 in 1958
e - No. 127 renumbered to 129 in 1959
f - Nos 171-9 rebodied by Crossley H56R in 1959
g - Nos. 29-42/7-57 refitted with Leyland engines and gearboxes in 1957-9
h - Nos. 94/6/9-100/3/4 rebuilt to O59R in 1970-2 and renumbered 5/6/1-4
i - Nos.249-52/4 rebuilt to O76F in 1977-9 and renumbered 7-11
j - ex Waddellⅰs Coaches, Lochwinnoch, new 1978

OLD PORTSMOUTH/DOCKYARD · SOUTHSEA/HAYLING FERRY

Via Broad Street, High Street, Pembroke Road, Clarence Pier and Clarence Esplanade or via The Hard, St. George's Road, Alexandra Road, Pier Road, Clarence Pier, Clarence Esplanade, South Parade Pier, Southsea Esplanade and Eastney Esplanade.

Operates according to traffic requirements and is liable to cancellation in unfavourable weather conditions.

Weekdays until 16th September 1972 and from 28th May 1973

			●		●		●				●		●		●		●		●
POINT, OLD PORTSMOUTH.......	......	1035	......	1105	......	1135	......	then at	05	...	35	...	1905	......	1935	......	2005	......	......
DOCKYARD ⌒ ≋..................	0948	1018	......	1048	......	1118	......	1148	these	...	18	...	48	......	1918	......	1948	......	2018	2048
Clarence Pier..................	0954	1024	1039	1054	1109	1124	1139	1154	minutes	09	24	39	54 until	1909	1924	1939	1954	2009	2024	2054
SOUTHSEA, South Parade Pier....	1000	1030	1045	1100	1115	1130	1145	1200	past	15	30	45	00	1915	1930	1945	2000	2015	2030	2100
HAYLING FERRY..................	1012	1042	......	1112	......	1142	......	1212	each hour	...	42	...	12	......	1942	......	2012♣	......	......	......

			●		●		●		●				●		●		●		●		●
HAYLING FERRY..................	......	1021	......	1051	then at	...	21	...	51	......	1821	......	1851	......	1921	......	1951	2021
SOUTHSEA, South Parade Pier....	0933	1003	1018	1033	1048	1103	these	18	33	48	03	1818	1833	1848	1903	1918	1933	1948	2003	2033
Clarence Pier..................	0939	1009	1024	1039	1054	1109	minutes	24	39	54	09 until	1824	1839	1854	1909	1924	1939	1954	2009	2039
DOCKYARD ⌒ ≋..................	0945	1015	......	1045	......	1115	past	...	45	...	15	......	1845	......	1915	......	1945	......	2015♣	2045
POINT, OLD PORTSMOUTH..........	......	1027	......	1057	......	each hour	27	...	57	...	1827	......	1857	......	1927	......	1957	......	......

Sundays until 10th September 1972 and from 27th May 1973

			●				●		●				●		●		●		●		●
POINT, OLD PORTSMOUTH.......	......	......	1040	......	then at	00	...	20	...	40	......	1900	......	1920	......	1940	......	2000	......	......
DOCKYARD ⌒ ≋..................	0948	1008	1028	......	1048	these	...	08	...	28	...	48	......	1908	......	1928	......	1948	......	2018	2038
Clarence Pier..................	0954	1014	1034	1044	1054	minutes	04	14	24	34	44	54 until	1904	1914	1924	1934	1944	1954	2004	2024	2044
SOUTHSEA, South Parade Pier....	1000	1020	1040	1050	1100	past	10	20	30	40	50	00	1910	1920	1930	1940	1950	2000	2010	2030	2050
HAYLING FERRY..................	1012	1032	1052	......	1112	each hour	...	32	...	52	...	12	......	1932	......	1952●	......	2012♣	......	......

			●		●		●				●		●		●		●		●		●
HAYLING FERRY..................	......	1001	......	1021	......	1041	then at	...	01	...	21	...	41	......	1901	......	1921	......	1941	2011
SOUTHSEA, South Parade Pier....	0933	0953	1013	1023	1033	1043	1053	these	03	13	23	33	43	53	1903	1913	1923	1933	1943	1953	2023
Clarence Pier..................	0939	0959	1019	1029	1039	1049	1059	minutes	09	19	29	39	49	59 until	1909	1919	1929	1939	1949	1959	2029
DOCKYARD ⌒ ≋..................	0945	1005	1025	......	1045	......	1105	past	12	...	25	...	45	...	05	......	1925	......	1945	......	2005♣	2035
POINT, OLD PORTSMOUTH..........	......	......	1032	......	1052	......	each hour	12	...	32	...	52	...	1912	......	1932	......	1952	......	......

CODE

♣—These journeys are extended (to Hayling Ferry or The Hard) until 2nd September 1972 only.
●—Operates until 2nd September 1972 only.   ⌒—Ferry connections to or from Isle of Wight and Gosport.   ≋—Near Railway Station.

Copies of two pages extracted from the 1972 timetable book. Above are the seasonal open-top timings and below a selection of special routes serving the Dockyard.

DOCKYARD SERVICES

Mondays to Fridays only

For Sunday morning services to the Dockyard, see pages 142-144.

FROM DEVON ROAD
Via Stubbington Avenue and Queen Street

DEVON ROAD.................................	0659
Green Lane, Copnor Road..................	0700
Stubbington Avenue, Copnor Road....	0702
North End, Junction......................	0706
DOCKYARD, Main Gate....................	0719

FROM DEVON ROAD
Via Chichester Road and Queen Street

DEVON ROAD.................................	0658
Green Lane, Copnor Road..................	0650
Stubbington Avenue, Copnor Road......	0700
Chichester Road, Copnor Road..........	0701
DOCKYARD, Main Gate....................	0714

FROM MILTON
Via Locksway Road and Goldsmith Ave.

MILTON, Furze Lane...........................	0656
Milton, White House.........................	0700
Fratton Bridge ≋..............................	0706
DOCKYARD, Unicorn Gate	0715

FROM WYMERING
Via Southampton Road and London Road

SEVENOAKS ROAD, Whitstable Road	0648
Wymering, Mablethorpe Road............	0658
Cosham, Railway Gates ≋..............	0701
Alexandra Park..............................	0708
DOCKYARD, Unicorn Gate	0717

FROM EASTNEY
Via Eastney Road, Devonshire Avenue, and Canal Walk

HIGHLAND ROAD, Eastney Road..............	0702
Devonshire Avenue, Eastney Road...........	0704
Fratton Bridge ≋..............................	0709
DOCKYARD, Unicorn Gate	0715

FROM EASTERN ROAD
Via St. Mary's Road and Queen Street

EASTERN ROAD, Langstone Road......	0700
St. Mary's Road, Milton Road.............	0703
DOCKYARD, Main Gate....................	0717

FROM STANLEY AVENUE
Via Tangier Road, New Road, Sultan Road and Herbert Street

STANLEY AVENUE.................................	0659
Copnor Bridge...................................	0702
DOCKYARD, Unicorn Gate	0717

CODE

≋—Adjoining or near Railway Station.

Epilogue

It was always intended that the story of the last 25 years would be outside the scope of this book but for the sake of completeness a brief résumé of events during this period is included. Unfortunately, it does not make happy reading and does not reflect particularly favourably on many of the people and organisations that have been involved. We have seen how Portsmouth City Transport Limited was formed from October 1986 and along with all other operators at the time, decisions had to be made in February that year as to the extent of the commercial network (ie, that to be operated without any subsidies at all) and one significant decision was that no services would be run on Sundays, unless obtained through the tendering process. The tender was actually won by Southdown Motor Services. Concurrent with all this was, of course, the sale of all the National Bus Company subsidiaries.

In 1987 a new operator trading as Red Admiral commenced competing with PCT Ltd. Red Admiral was jointly owned by Southampton Citybus, the trading name of the former Southampton City Transport, and the Badgerline group based on the former Bristol Omnibus operations (who subsequently merged with Grampian to form FirstBus), although their share in Red Admiral was sold to Citybus within a year. Early in 1988 Portsmouth City Council, still the owners of PCT, decided to sell their bus company. The successful bidder was Southern Vectis from the Isle of Wight but an inability to finalise the terms of the sale resulted in the proposed sale collapsing and in June 1988 it was announced by the City Council that the company had been sold to a consortium of which shareholding was 75% Southampton Citybus and 25% Portsmouth City Transport employees. Interestingly, this was the first privatisation of a former municipal operator and the deal included a three year lease on the Eastney depot. The new undertaking commenced trading as Portsmouth CityBus and Red Admiral became a subsidiary, utilising mainly minibuses. However, it was still not free from competition as Southdown, which had been sold to its management in October 1987, and People's Provincial, which had been the subject of a unique Employee Share Ownership Plan in May 1987, both had a strong presence in the city.

It was perhaps no surprise when the rather precarious financial position of Portsmouth CityBus resulted in its sale to Stagecoach in October 1989. Stagecoach decided to merge the operations in Portsmouth with those of Southdown, which it had bought earlier in the same year and commenced trading as Southdown Portsmouth. It decided to base its operations at Eastney and accordingly closed its Hilsea depot. As with several similar acquisitions at the time, the Monopolies and Mergers Commission decided to investigate Stagecoach's purchase of Portsmouth CityBus but concluded in July 1990 that while the takeover was against the public interest, it had not caused any adverse effects and that there should be no divestment. Both Portsmouth City Council and Hampshire County Council, together with the employees' trade unions and several bus user groups, supported this view as it was recognised that it was unlikely that the business would have remained viable in the long term. However, the Secretary of State for Trade and Industry, Nicholas Ridley, who had long been regarded as the architect of bus deregulation, overruled the MMC decision and directed that Stagecoach should divest itself of the Portsmouth operations. Accordingly, in January 1991 this business was sold to Transit Holdings, a group formed following the privatisation of Devon General, and renamed it Portsmouth Transit.

Transit Holdings modus operandi, which had been based on the Exeter model which it had established under the NBC, was to operate high frequency minibus services and it commenced to apply this principle to Portsmouth. Branded routes running in the City area became Blue Admiral services and those outside Red Admiral. Initially, the premises at Eastney were used but since they were soon to become unavailable, it established premises at Hilsea for the former and premises at Havant for the latter. People's Provincial, meanwhile, recognising that the use of minibuses was not universally popular, expanded its operations believing that a significant number of passengers preferred conventionally sized buses. People's Provincial was sold to FirstGroup (as FirstBus had now become) in October 1995 but by now Transit Holdings had begun to contract and it was hardly a surprise when they too sold out to FirstGroup in 1996, consolidation of the two organisations coming soon afterwards.

When First purchased Southampton CityBus from its employees in 1997, they having bought it from the Council four years earlier, the whole was later to be merged as First Hampshire and Dorset and based at Portswood, once a tram depot for Southampton Corporation. This company was not to be without its own problems; in 2006 the Traffic Commissioner fined the company for poor punctuality in Portsmouth. What would Ben Hall have made of it all?

Acknowledgements

The assistance of David Janes, without whose help this book could not have been completed, has already been acknowledged, but many others have provided invaluable assistance.

David Packer answered an early call for help, and John and Mark Senior have used, as ever, their technical expertise to convert the assembled material into an acceptable publication, not forgetting David and Mary Shaw who have once again proof-read the manuscript to its benefit although any errors that remain are mine.

The book has benefited from a long-standing arrangement in relation to the maps, but I am especially grateful to David Bowler for his permission to use one from a series of maps that have been produced for his forthcoming book on Portsmouth's trolleybuses.

Almost without exception, the colour photographs have come from the collection of David Janes and I am again grateful for his generosity.

As indicated in the introduction, the catalyst for this book was the donation to Venture Publications of a large photographic collection. Unfortunately, many of these pictures have no indication of the photographer. Even where that is recorded, there is no way of knowing whether they are still the copyright holder. Whenever possible the photographer has been acknowledged, but apologies must be offered if this is not always the case.

Photographic credits

ABC	Alan Cross
ADP	David Packer
ADPC	David Packer collection
DAPJ	David Janes
FWY	Fred York
GAT	GA Tucker
JAS	John A Senior
PT	Peter Trevaskis
RGF	Reg Funnell
RM	Roy Marshall
RGR	Bob Rowe
STA	Senior Transport Archive
TVR	TV Runnacles

Bibliography

Ian Allan BBF South Eastern Area (1st and 2nd Editions, 1956 & 1958 respectively)
Portsmouth Corporation Transport (Buses Illustrated No. 115 – October 1964) THJ Dethridge
Trolleybuses of Portsmouth (Janes & Funnell) 1969 (February)
PSV Circle publication PK5 (July 1969) and PH14 (February 1997)
Solent Transport Trust - *City of Portsmouth illustrated fleet list* (Viewfinder) 1978
Fares Please (Eric Watts) 1987
Southdown Motor Services Vol 1 (Venture) Colin Morris 1994
Portsmouth's Tramways (Middleton Press) 1996
Gosport & Horndean Tramways (Middleton Press) 1997
Local Transport History compiled by Peter Gould.
Portsmouth City Transport - Buses Extra 65 (Roy Marshall)
The Evening News, Portsmouth

For many years Portsmouth's only preserved tram, No. 84, was to be found at the back of North End depot. It was a former horse tram and was rebuilt for the electric system in 1904 being withdrawn by 1936. It is seen in the upper picture at Eastney depot, prior to further perambulations around Hampshire.

This 1919 Thornycroft motorbus has been in preservation since 1939, having served as a petrol tanker for the department from 1927 when its passenger-carrying duties ceased. During the latter part of the 20th century it was frequently to be seen at bus rallies in Hampshire, here at Netley Park, Southampton. It now carries its correct (original) fleet number 10, having masqueraded as No. 1 for some considerable time.

Portsmouth's first trolleybus is the only pre-war one preserved and is seen in the upper picture outside the City Museum. During the 1960s it was on display at the Montague Motor Museum at Beaulieu. Restored as No. 201, the fleet number it carried from 1938, it is a 1934 AEC 661T with English Electric body. The livery is a mix of pre-war and post-war styles.

A large batch of Craven-bodied AECs entered service in 1936/7 and the final ones in service lasted to the penultimate month of trolleybus operation. Number 286 is seen crossing Guildhall Square under much simplified overhead in its last month of operation.

The first Leyland TD4s entered service in 1935 and four of them completed over 36 years service as a result of their conversion to open-top configuration in 1953-5. Number 117, subsequently renumbered 6, is seen here at the Hayling Ferry terminus with parts of the Mulberry Harbour, used in the Normandy D-Day landings in 1944, in the background.

Leyland themselves provided a small number of bodies on their TD4 chassis in 1935, these being examples of the Lancashire company's early metal-framed output, and their six-bay window arrangements and V-fronts looked a little dated when compared with the English Electric design.

Pictured during the last few weeks of service No. 313, delivered in 1950 and now to be found in preservation at the East Anglia Transport Museum, travels along Southsea Terrace where tram lines, disused for 27 years, remained with only tar covering the metals. This was one of 15 BUT 9611Ts with Burlingham bodies which were Portsmouth's only post-war trolleybuses.

An unusual working after the conversion of services 7-8 and 11-12 to motorbus operation which continued until the closure of the system was the sole Friday-only short-working to Green Lane of a service 5 bus, which needless to say attracted the attention of enthusiasts. Here No. 307 reverses into Compton Road on the by then once a week manoeuvre.

The combination of Crossley bodies on Daimler chassis was not unusual in some parts of the country, but was certainly unique on the south coast, where Portsmouth's nine wartime CWA6s had their original Duple bodies replaced by the Stockport builder in 1959. Number 176 is pictured here.

Almost equally rare were two Reading-bodied Leyland PD1As which entered service in 1947 and which were joined by four more the following year. The first, No. 199, is seen here on Copnor Road, Hilsea in 1966 by which time it was confined to driver tuition duties.

With a background of North End depot, the first Weymann-bodied Leyland PD1 No. 180 stands in the summer sun in June 1966 just a month before withdrawal.

All-Crossley No. 56 of 1949 gave nearly 18 years service to the city and is pictured here in Blackfriars Road on service 18, a number used at that point be successively trams, trolleybuses and motorbuses.

Portsmouth operated no less than 65 Leyland PD2 models and the first 25 were bodied by the chassis builder. Blackfriars Road is again the location, this time with No. 66 heading for Eastney.

The subsequent PD2s were bodied by Metro-Cammell and No. 92 was captured on camera from the footbridge at Northern Road Cosham.

Underfloor-engined single-deckers, intended to be operated by a driver only, first entered service in 1960 and were Leyland Tiger Cubs with Weymann dual-door bodies, represented here by No. 21 on service 24 at Cosham.

The Tiger Cubs were followed by Leyland Leopards, also with bodies by Weymann, and No. 135 is seen on service 16 at Alexandra Park, about to depart for Eastney, in March 1964. This service was a direct replacement for the erstwhile trolleybus route which was discontinued in April 1960.

After the arrival of the Leyland Leopards, delivery commenced of the first Leyland Atlanteans in 1963. Originally intended to also have been bodied by Weymann, they were in fact built in Birmingham by Metro-Cammell and 35 were delivered that year, followed by ten in 1964 and nine in 1966. In the upper picture No. 224, from the first batch, is seen passing the Southdown garage at Hilsea, whilst below No. 245, delivered in 1964, is seen in Leigh Park.

A further 26 single-deckers, also suitable for one-man-operation, arrived in 1967. This time they were the Leyland Panther Cub model, bodywork for which was split between Marshall and Metro-Cammell. Pictured above on its first day in service, No. 158 was one of the Marshall examples.

The next buses to enter the fleet, in 1969, were the first AEC buses to do so since 1931. They were twelve AEC Swifts, also bodied by Marshall, and they originally carried the same style of livery as No. 158 above. Seen after the revised livery was applied is No.179, outside Eastney depot and at the opposite end of the 16 service from that shown on page 136.

The years 1971/2 saw more Atlanteans arrive, but they created something of a surprise, as they were bodied as single-deckers by Seddon of Oldham, Lancashire. They totalled twelve and No. 194 is depicted, travelling along Northern Road at Cosham.

The first over-all advertising bus materialised in 1971, when No. 249 appeared promoting the Tricorn Centre. Covered in hundreds of facial characters, it had to be seen to appreciate its dreadful impact, but thankfully it only ran in this guise for four months before becoming the first bus to wear the new livery, in December 1971. Later it was to be converted to open-top.

The original 1935-delivered open-top fleet had received the livery seen above in 1968 and No. 5 is at Bransbury Park with blinds set for the other open-top service to Hayling Ferry numbered 26, a somewhat rare and elusive animal.

In due course the open-top Leyland TD4s were replaced by newer Leyland PD2s, six of the 1956 delivery being converted in 1971/2. In 1977 their livery was modified to reflect the Queen's Silver Jubilee year. Number 4, originally No. 104, is seen in Southsea, with South Parade Pier in the background.

From 1972 the body contract for the Atlantean double-deckers was changed to Alexanders of Falkirk and a total of 90 such units were to eventually enter service, with No. 296 of 1975 seen here at The Hard.

Additional single-deck requirements were met by delivery of the ubiquitous Leyland National, of which Portsmouth took 14 in 1976 and No. 107 is in Highland Road, Eastney.

In due course Portsmouth's second generation of open-top buses became due for retiring and their replacements were five 1966 Atlanteans which were rebuilt between 1977 and 1979, and this enabled all the department's services to be operated with a driver only. Former No. 252 became No.10 in open-top form and is seen here at The Hard Interchange soon after re-entering service after rebuilding.

Subsequent all-over advertising buses were perhaps more tastefully designed than the example shown on page 139 and as an example Alexander-bodied Leyland No. 266 carried this promotion for The News, an organisation aware of the need for good design where matters concerning sales were concerned; it ran from 1979 until 1982.

The opening of the Continental Ferry Port in 1976 subsequently gave rise to a bespoke service between the Harbour Railway Station and the port, and this led to the use of luggage trailers, which were towed by the single-deck Atlanteans, as illustrated by No. 188 leaving The Hard Interchange. The trailers came from the British Airways Board in 1979 having been originally used at Heathrow.

The last double-deck buses to be purchased by the City of Portsmouth Passenger Transport Department in 1980 represented yet another builder new to the undertaking. The ten Leyland AN68s numbered 345-54 receiving East Lancs 73-seat dual-door bodywork. All the 1980 deliveries had rather appropriate registration letters for a city with such a large Naval connection.

Three more Leyland Nationals entered the fleet in 1980 and besides being the first Mark 2 examples to be received, also had dual-purpose seating for 40 and were the first vehicles to revert to a single door for 14 years. The first one, No. 98 is seen in Isambard Brunel Road.

Three Dennis Lancets with Wadham Stringer bodies arrived in 1982. The first, No. 95, GTP 95X, had a dual-purpose 33-seat body; the other two, Nos. 96/7, had 35-seat bus bodies.